FINANCING THE ENDTIME HARVEST —GOD'S WAY

BY
DR. JOHN F. AVANZINI

BOX 1057
HURST, TEXAS USA
76053

ISBN 0-941117-04-9
Printed in the United States of America.

This book is lovingly dedicated to

PATRICIA ANN AVANZINI,

my partner in ministry and in life.

CONTENTS

FOREWORD

One of the biggest lies the devil has dumped on you and me and the entire Body of Christ—is that **Christians should be poor.** Poverty produces piety, holiness, and humility, the lie goes on. Besides, wasn't Jesus poor? Satan wants us to believe that because we have renounced the world and all its "riches" (as the song goes), we should just be poor and "hold out, faithful to the end."

Some years ago a few men of God began to teach that this is, indeed, a lie from Satan, because the Word of God teaches we should **PROSPER.**

WHAM! Satan launched such a vicious counterattack it is still dangerous to use the word **PROSPERITY** in some public Christian meetings! The teaching on prosperity was denounced from the pulpits, and whole denominations took up the chant, "Down with prosperity!"

Oh, it was all right to have **"Spiritual Prosperity,"** but we were told to forget any idea that Christians should have financial or material prosperity. After all, that was precisely what was wrong with the Church: "Too much focus on materialism is leading us away from God."

Then came the ridiculous charge that Christians were using the Word to confess Cadillacs and all kinds of other "worldly excesses!" Some good teachers and preachers were so mercilessly maligned that many gave up this important message and moved on to safer and far less controversial subjects, while Satan danced in glee to see all the bloodletting among the people of God.

"Mission accomplished" was flashed back to the devil's headquarters in hell.

But in the heat, lightning, fire and smoke from this fruitless debate, most of us missed the whole point God was trying to get across! It is found in Deuteronomy, chapter eight:

> But thou shalt remember the Lord Thy God: for it is
> he that giveth thee power to get wealth, that he may
> establish his covenant . . .
>
> *Deuteronomy 8:18a*

I believe the main reason we have not already established the Kingdom of God on earth is simply this: we have accepted the lie of Satan that says Christians should be poor!

Satan fears more than anything else that God's people will get hold of the resources of this world because, he knows that when we do, we will "establish His (God's) covenant."

8

And what was this covenant spoken about by Moses? That covenant is found in Genesis, chapters 12 through 17. God promises Abraham that through him **"ALL THE FAMILIES OF THE EARTH WOULD BE BLESSED"**; many other things were also promised:

1. Abraham would be multiplied exceedingly,
2. He would be a father of many nations,
3. He would become exceedingly fruitful (wealthy),
4. All the land of Canaan would be given to him, and
5. Jehovah would be God to him and his children forever.

Time and space do not permit a full teaching here on the Abrahamic Covenant, but the bottom line is simply this:

> *God's covenant promised Abraham he would produce a family through which a Savior would come who would repossess Planet Earth from the devil and establish God's Kingdom!*

Please put this into your spirit: there is nothing wrong in desiring or having wealth if your purpose and motive is to **establish the Kingdom of God!** That's God's perfect plan, and we missed it!

Of course, Satan had a few phonies who professed great spirituality but used and abused the Prosperity message and nearly ruined it for all of us. Even some of God's real people got off the track here and there; there are always excesses whenever a new or renewed truth of God comes forward.

But thank God for a few early pioneers like R.G. Le Tourneau, Andrew Carnegie, W.W. Kellog, and J.C. Penney who led the way by proving that there is nothing wrong with wealth if it is used to establish the Kingdom of God. Without them, we would not be as far along as we are now in establishing the Kingdom.

Where were we—the people of God—back in the early 1950's when the Federal Communication Commission allocated all of the TV station licenses for America? I'll tell you where we were—we were back in our little 2 x 4 churches singing "Hold the Fort" and preaching that to be spiritual you had to be poor! And while we were poor, the devil took all of the TV stations into his hellish control! It wasn't until the 1960's and 1970's that a few of God's people woke up and started repossessing the airwaves which were ours "by covenant" all the time!

Are you getting hold of this?

Up to now (with rare exceptions) we have established the Kingdom of God with the widow's mite—small sacrificial gifts—and praise God for them! We would be nowhere without them. Again

9

and again I have seen God's "faithful people" come through when there was a need or a chance to buy another TV station. How I love and thank God for these precious people everyday.

But **now**, we are on the home stretch.

God is looking for a people–a whole new breed–who will become partners with Him! These are people God can trust with wealth–people who are good stewards through whom He can establish His covenant, His Kingdom!

In this exciting book by Dr. John Avanzini, we have key-after-key spelled out from the Word of God showing us we can take the resources of this world and use them to establish God's Kingdom!

Let's read them and then **do them** in Jesus' Name!

Paul F. Crouch, Sr.
President/Founder
Trinity Broadcasting Network, Inc.

INTRODUCTION

Child of God, what a wonderful experience you are going to have, ...

AS YOU BEGIN ...

TO EXPERIENCE ...

– A TRANSFORMATION PROCESS IN YOUR MIND!

Keep this in mind: Your new mentality will not come immediately. Oh, I know that in this "instant" society we have come to expect "instant" answers. Even Quaker makes instant oatmeal!

But, no one has invented an instant way to cause you to become a prosperous Christian. Your mental transformation process must occur in a Biblical progression.

For precept must be upon precept,
precept upon precept;
line upon line, line upon line;
here a little, and there a little:

Isaiah 28: 10

This is exactly how **God's prosperity mentality will invade and transform your mind** – concept by concept, precept upon precept, line upon line, here a little, there a little.

As you read the challenging new concepts contained in the lessons in this book, you may question some of these concepts. They may seem so dramatic, and so different from your present beliefs that you may question whether or not they are really biblical.

Well, child of God, there is a special scripture just for that questioning feeling. Let it be your guide as you undertake this thought-jarring, life-transforming experience.

*To the law and to the testimony; **if they speak not** **according to this word, it is because there is no** **light in them.***

Isaiah 8:20

Go ahead and question the new thoughts I submit to you.

Double-check the scriptures I quote in this book. Study their context.

If this is to be a life-changing experience for you, you must **PARTICIPATE IN THE PROCESS.**

1. Read.
2. Question.
3. Research.
4. **Then** change.

11

Always remember that when you deal with God's mind on any matter, it is very common for His precepts and conclusions to be very different from our own. God puts us on notice of this possibility:

> Let the wicked forsake his way, and the unrighteous
> man his thoughts: and let him return unto the Lord,
> and he will have mercy upon him; and to our God, for
> he will abundantly pardon.
> For my thoughts are not your thoughts, neither are
> your ways my ways, saith the Lord.
> For as the heavens are higher than the earth, so are
> my ways higher than your ways, and my thoughts
> than your thoughts.
>
> *Isaiah 55: 7-9*

Child of God, here is your challenge:

The concepts in God's word are sometimes going to be very different from the current concepts in your mind.

Why? Your mind has certain unscriptural concepts **programmed into it,** and those programs have been reinforced daily, and gone virtually **unchallenged** for many years. Remember, they were put into your mind line upon line, precept upon precept, here a little, there a little.

Therefore, they must be removed the very same way.

That is why God led me to create this book as a living tool to be used by the Holy Spirit, lesson upon lesson, to lead you into a new breakthrough mentality in your finances.

Remember – as you read these lessons, it is not enough to just put new information into your mind. We must get the old, erroneous, non-scriptural information you have stored up out of your mind forever.

This false information comes from many well-meaning people.

Some of your concepts came from your parents.

Some of your concepts came from your teachers.

Some of your concepts came from pastors, preachers and Sunday school teachers.

Some of your concepts came from the music you enjoy.

But, wherever your concepts come from, realize now that from virtually every place you go, and everything you experience, concepts and ideas are instilled in you – some are scriptural, some are not. You must now begin to regulate the input of concepts into your mind by feeding it only good Bible concepts regularly.

As you PARTICIPATE in this mind transformation, please do not hesitate to accept these new concepts just because they may not come into agreement with what you have already learned over the years.

JUST MAKE IT YOUR CRITERIA THAT THESE NEW CONCEPTS MUST AGREE WITH THE PRECIOUS WORD OF GOD!

Freely question and examine the concepts in this book; be absolutely sure they agree with scripture. Then accept them and begin to put them into practice.

Let me make you a promise. I will not give you any new concept without also giving you the scripture reference to support it. Please note: If you would demand this same scriptural standard in every aspect of your life, you would experience a whole new mentality, not just in the realm of God's finances, but in virtually every area of your life. Total transformation would come in your health, happiness, sanctification, and in other areas too numerous to write here.

If you would, from this day forward, insist that every concept you learn lines up directly with God's Word, then, child of God,

- You would soon have a new mentality about the second coming of Jesus Christ,
- You would soon have a new mentality about the holiness doctrine,
- You would soon have a new mentality about consecration and dedication, and
- You would soon have a new mentality on how to be a good Christian parent!

If you strictly demanded that the only things you allowed to stick in your mind would be the things that line up with the Word of God, you would find yourself not easily misguided by new doctrines that come from many sources around you. You would find yourself rising up out of your defeated or near-defeated circumstances, and moving into new bold adventures for your God.

Casting down imaginations, and every high thing that exalteth itself against the knowledge of God, and bringing into captivity every thought to the obedience of Christ;

II Corinthians 10: 5

Notice that the process outlined in this verse is precisely the one we follow in this book: **Cast down** imaginations that are

13

against the knowledge of God, and **bring into** captivity every thought into the obedience of Christ.

It is time for you to become the dynamic, surging force God intended you to be when he redeemed you with His blood and the word of truth!

Child of God, if there is going to be transformation in **any** area of your life, it must first be cleansed of the unscriptural principles and be reprogrammed to line up with God's original intentions in His precious Word. As your mind is "renewed," **you will become what God intended for you to be** in the very beginning, when He planned for you to have victories and conquests as you serve Him.

In this book, **FINANCING THE ENDTIME HARVEST— GOD'S WAY**, I believe God will TRANSFORM your thinking in the area of finances, and direct you right back to the plan He intended for you in the very beginning!

Remember, if there is going to be a change in your thinking in the area of prosperity, you will have to **PARTICIPATE IN THE PROCESS.** Allow God to gradually BREAKTHROUGH your old concepts and your old ideas. You must be willing to allow God's plan for your DIVINE PROSPERITY to crowd out the devil's plan for your mediocrity, failure, and continual insufficiency.

Lay firm hold on this—**the battle is in your mind.**

You are what you think you are. God's word tells us:

For as he thinketh in his heart, so is he:

Proverbs 23: 7 a

When thoughts enter your mind, they soon become deeply rutted into your God-given computer. Once a concept becomes part of your thinking process, it will guide you like a silent homing device that always brings you to the same, predetermined conclusion.

For various reasons, you may have already reached a "predetermined conclusion" that **Christians should be poor.** If you do not allow the scripture and God's Spirit to break through your old thinking, you will continue to believe the same old unscriptural conclusion you did BEFORE you read this book, and you will remain without enough of what you need.

Have you ever heard the expression, "set in concrete?" The longer concrete sits, the harder it gets. After five or ten years, it is much more difficult to break up a concrete slab than it is soon after the slab hardens.

Time actually makes concrete harder to break.

Time does the same thing with the unscriptural, unchallenged concepts in your mind. The longer they sit, unquestioned and undisturbed, the harder they are to break. Remember, God does

14

not want your false concepts to harden and strengthen their grip on you. His Word tells you to cast them down, and to break unscriptural strongholds off of your mind.

As you read this book, I believe God will perform a great, "concept-shattering" BREAKTHROUGH in your life. He wants to break those old concepts which are "set in concrete" in your mind, and put HIS MIND into you. After all, scripture encourages us to make our minds like the mind of Christ.

> *Let this mind be in you, which was also in Christ Jesus.*
> Philippians 2:5

Notice, the verse does not say that the Mind of Christ will instantly POP into your mind at the time you are saved. The Word says "**LET** this mind be in you."

You must **PARTICIPATE IN THE PROCESS!**

God's Word also talks about being "TRANSFORMED by the renewing" of your mind:

> *And be not conformed to this world: **but be ye TRANSFORMED by the RENEWING of your mind,** that ye may prove what is that good, and acceptable, and perfect, will of God.*
> Romans 12:2

Notice, it does not say you will receive an instant, Quaker-oatmeal type of transformation.

It does say there are some new dynamic thoughts Jesus wants to put into your mind, and those new thoughts will give you a new kind of life.

But, child of God, **YOU PARTICIPATE IN THE PROCESS!** Why does God want you to undergo this process? " . . . That ye may prove (literally, that you may have first-hand knowledge of) what is that good, and acceptable, and perfect, will of God."

As your bold new adventure begins, many of you probably want to believe that God desires for you to "have the best," but you are afraid.

Perhaps you are thinking:

"Oh, Brother John, I want this process to work so much. I want to believe in new, powerful, prosperous thoughts. I desire to have the abundance God speaks about in His precious Word, and to be able to freely give to the special projects God puts on my heart. I want to be able to travel to spiritually nurturing conventions. I want to support Christian television, mission endeavors, and many other powerful ministries. I'm tired of the never-ending financial struggle; I want to be able to give generously to my church, *and* to my family."

15

Child of God, you can do it!

But, you must first understand everything runs in cycles. If you do not grasp this, you will miss everything that has to do with the abundance God wants to give to you.

A "cycle" simply means that things are running in a circle – just like the dog chasing his own tail. The harder he tries to catch it, the more futile the chase seems.

If you are now in the cycle of insufficiency, you will continue to "chase your tail" and come up with more and more insufficiency. You will not have enough to give properly, and in not giving enough, you will not receive enough. In not receiving, you will not have enough to give properly.

Somehow you must break out of that cycle!

This is why God has led you to this book, **FINANCING THE ENDTIME HARVEST – GOD'S WAY.** As you accept the God-given truths in this book, under the influence of the Holy Spirit, you will be led into a bold new cycle of abundance with God. You see, until you become a great receiver, you will not be able to become a great giver, and until you become a great giver, you will not be a great receiver.

Something has to change.

Something has to move.

The insufficiency cycle has to be broken, and the abundance cycle must be started.

And the thing that has to move is that old thinking process that continues to bring you to the insufficiency you have lived with for so long. But now, let Jesus make all things new! God does want you to prosper! So from this moment on, lesson upon lesson, precept upon precept, let Him purge out the old insufficiency and replace it with the new abundance He has for you.

Now once and for all break the cycle of insufficiency!

Look at what the apostle John "prays" in III John 2:

Beloved, I wish (pray) above all things that thou mayest prosper and be in health, even as thy soul prospereth.

My, what a wonderful thing John prayed for you. He could have prayed that you would learn to live with shortage and insufficiency, or that you might be content in your poverty. He could have prayed that you might have the ability to scrimp and scrape in your hour of need.

But no, instead John speaks of a great, bold, powerful move in your life, a "God-kind" of move, the kind that would bring you . . .

16

- Out of the cycle of lack, and into the cycle of abundance.
- Out of the cycle of want, and into the cycle of more than enough.

Child of God, aren't you really tired of being continuously short of the material substances you need to fully and completely obey God in the many wonderful ways He wants you to give?

Now, before you begin this powerful, stirring process of prosperity breakthrough thinking, let me share with you a few, final thoughts.

God never gives you a vision that is larger than what your finances **would be** (notice I didn't say **are**) at the time of your vision, **if** you had obeyed Him every time in the past when He told you to give, and if you had given the amount He said to give.

Your current financial condition is determined by your past obedience in giving.

Your future financial condition will be determined by your obedience today.

You see, you do not receive from God in accordance with your need.

Please do not run to Philippians 4:19 and begin to quote it to me:

But my God shall supply all your needs according to
his riches in glory by Christ Jesus.

That promise does not start in the 19th verse; it actually starts in the 15th verse, where Paul speaks to the Philippians who were the only mission givers among the early churches. Because of their regular support of Paul's ministry, Paul spoke this blessing upon them.

The blessing of Philippians 4:19 is not the property of the whole church world. It applies only to those who regularly support world missions!

God is not moved by need. If He was, He would only bless the areas of the world where the need is greatest.

He would bless the starving in India.

He would send food and rain on portions of Africa, where men, women, and little children are dying by the tens of thousands amid severe drought and famine.

He would move only on skid row, and not in the highrise penthouses in the very same city.

But many times God moves in the most affluent situations. You see, hard as it may seem for your old mentality to accept, God is not moved by need; God is moved by faith. The reason God is moved by our faith is because true faith brings us to **OBEDIENCE.**

17

You see, everytime God tells you to give a certain amount, you must release the amount he tells you to give, whether it is in your church, for a Christian telethon or a great mission offering. God is not only raising money for the "vision" or outreach to which you are giving, He is also raising FUTURE MONEY for you and for the vision He plans for you to accomplish for Him.

You see, He is teaching you the PROCESS of sowing so you can have an abundant harvest when you need it so you can move into your special vision, and have your special need met.

Child of God, if you start now, understand that there will be a little time of catching up to God's prosperity for your life. Remember, you did not come to your present problem in a day. So do not expect God to get you out of it in a day, because we never reap the same day we sow. It will take a season for your new prosperity crops to become ready to harvest.

Remember, the Bible says that if you sow, **in due season**, YOU WILL REAP!

If YOU cast your bread on the water, **in a number of days,** it will come back to you again; God says the blessings will overtake you!

God's Word is pregnant with promises of reaping the harvest if you are faithful in sowing.

So, child of God, begin now.

Make yourself a promise.

Make your God a promise.

Each morning read one of the lessons in this book. Do not go to sleep in the evening without once again reading that same lesson. If you can, read the lesson a time or two during the day, and meditate on them through the day. Spaced repetition is proven to be the most effective type of learning. Speak the concepts out loud, if possible, all day, as often as you can. If you will dedicate yourself to this task, then the Word of God will begin to live in you in the realm of prosperity. Your new prosperity mentality will bring you the riches of the Gentiles, and put in your hands the keys to the treasure house of God. You can learn to finance the endtime harvest in God's way!

Let's keep the proper perspective: God doesn't want to prosper you so you can lavish it on yourself like much of the current teaching tells us. However, God will prosper you so you can be a potent, effective force in REACHING THE WORLD for Jesus Christ through your giving.

In fact, the Bible speaks of a ministry – a special grace for giving – so we can literally become "God's bankers," those who will finance God's work with the money with which God has prospered them.

Now don't get discouraged. God will bless you abundantly as you move into this mentality of abundance. God wants you to enjoy and "eat" from that which you bring forth. God said the servant is worthy of hire, and He will see that you have more than enough.

> *But remember this—if you give little, you will get little. A farmer who plants just a few seeds will get only a small crop, but if he plants much, he will reap much. Every one must make up his own mind as to how much he should give. Don't force anyone to give more than he really wants to, for cheerful givers are the ones God prizes.*
>
> *Yes, God will give you much so that you can give away much, and when we take your gifts to those who need them they will break out into thanksgiving and praise to God for your help.*
>
> II Corinthians 6,7,&11
TLB

Keep this in mind: You can't be God's banker with a poverty mentality. You can't be God's banker if you are shy and ashamed and embarrassed about boldly taking a portion of the wealth and finances of the world and putting them into your control. You cannot be God's banker unless you know God wants you to prosper and know His laws of prosperity can apply to your daily life.

Child of God, you can BREAK THROUGH in your financial situation if you will hear God clearly as He speaks to you from the pages of His Bible. I promise you that in this book I will not give you my thoughts. I will only give you the thoughts of God that are written clearly in His Word.

So now, if you are ready, make this commitment. Please pray this prayer aloud:

"Dear God, I make a solemn commitment with you today. I promise you, Lord, that each day I will digest one of these lessons, and your wonderful truths will become a part of my life. Lord, I know that as I draw nigh to You, in this new mentality, you will draw nigh to me, even as the scripture says.

"Oh God, I thank you that I can come to You, knowing You are a covenant-making God. I now make this covenant with You, with the angels as a witness.

"Lord, I will be faithful in this covenant, and I know that You will, in Jesus' Name, be faithful in Your promises to me. Amen."

My prayer, from the very beginning when I started writing this book, until now as you read it, is that you will experience a new, prosperity mentality. I pray that your mind will be turned upside down by Jesus Christ through His precious Word, and that all your old concepts will be replaced by a fresh, new, God-given prosperity mentality.

One final note to the Reader

You will no doubt skim through the pages of this book before the designated day you read each daily lesson. Please DO NOT let this stop you from reading one lesson each morning, and then rereading the lesson again that night. Without this line upon line, precept upon precept method of learning, you will not experience nearly as strong an impression upon your mind.

Also note that couples and families can read these lessons together, or they can be studied in a daily Bible study at work, in the neighborhood, or at school. For the best results, however, each person should have a copy of this book for notes and rereading each lesson in the morning and evening.

Dr. John F. Avanzini

SECTION ONE:
POVERTY OR PROSPERITY?

Lesson 1: Poverty or PROSPERITY — *the choice* is YOURS!

Satan has lied to the saints!

For too long the devil has told us this lie:

"Some people are destined to be poor, and some people are destined to be rich, and there's nothing you can do about either circumstance."

Child of God, this satanic lie has crippled the finances of individual Christians, and Christian ministries, for far too long! It is time we learn the truth! There are three main reasons why this destructive statement is a lie:

1. It is a lie . . . because God is not a respecter of persons.

> *Then Peter opened his mouth, and said, Of a truth I perceive that God is no respecter of persons:*
> *Acts 10: 34*

God did not predetermine who would be rich and who would be poor. He simply created His Spiritual Laws, and freely gives them to everyone. Every person then has a choice — to implement the Laws of Poverty, or to implement God's Spiritual Laws of Prosperity.

2. It is a lie . . . because God's desire is that you prosper.

This is plainly stated in scripture.

> ***Beloved, I wish above all things that thou mayest prosper*** *and be in health, even as thy soul prospereth.*
> *III John 2*

Prosperity, not poverty, is God's intention for your life.

3. It is a lie . . . because God has given you the power to get wealth!

> *But thou shalt **remember the Lord thy God: for it is he that giveth thee power to get wealth,** that he may establish his covenant which he sware unto thy fathers, as it is this day.*
> *Deuteronomy 8:18*

God would not give you the **power to get wealth** if He did not intend for you to USE THAT POWER and become wealthy! The decision to live in poverty or to live in prosperity is YOURS!

God has already cast His vote – **HE WANTS YOU TO BE PROSPEROUS.** Make your life-changing decision today to reject the destructive laws of poverty and to accept your God-given rights under God's Law of Abundance.

Remember:

- God is no respecter of persons. (Acts 10:34)
- God wants you to prosper. (III John 2)
- God gives you the power to get wealth. (Deuteronomy 8:18)

Lesson 2: The God-given Laws of Poverty *and* Prosperity

God has created spiritual laws that determine who has wealth, and who will remain poor.

That's right!

The laws of poverty and the laws of wealth are authored by the same God who created the law of gravity, and ALL of His laws work every single time they are applied.

An apple will always fall to the ground. That's God's Law of Gravity.

A person will become rich or poor – by following God's laws.

One of the **THE LAWS OF POVERTY** simply says, "If you are lazy, or if you do not understand your task, – then your fields will not bring forth abundance; they will only grow thorns and nettles (a symbol of the unproductive yield that brings about want and insufficiency)."

*I went by the field of the **slothful,** and by the vineyard
of the man **void of understanding;**
And, lo, it was all grown over with thorns, and
nettles had covered the face thereof, and the stone wall
thereof was broken down.*

Proverbs 24: 30, 31

One of God's **LAWS OF PROSPERITY** simply says, "If you are not lazy, and can work without supervision, you will receive a bountiful supply."

*Go to the ant, thou sluggard; consider her ways, and
be wise:*

22

*Which **having no guide, overseer, or ruler,***
Provideth her meat in the summer, and gathereth her
food in the harvest.

Proverbs 6: 6-8

Do you feel the old concepts in your mind starting to fall away? Right now you are probably saying, "But Brother John, I resent the implication that I'm lazy. I'm not, and yet I'm continuously without the abundance that I need."

Remember, I have only touched on **two** factors in a poverty mentality today – laziness, and the lack of proper understanding to perform a task.

There are many other laws.

Just allow your PROCESS OF PARTICIPATION to start. If you do not become "set in concrete," you will experience a gradual transformation of your thoughts into **YOUR PROSPERITY MENTALITY.**

Do as the Bereans did in the first century: they received the Word readily, and searched the scriptures daily to see if these things were so! (Acts 17:10-11)

Lesson 3: God's Law of Reward

There are four "R's" which govern the laws of poverty and prosperity: Reward, Release, Receiving, and Reaping. Today, I want you to think about **REWARD.**

God's Spiritual Law of Reward simply states:
For the labourer is worthy of his hire (reward).

Luke 10:7b

Your employer is not doing you any special favor by writing you a paycheck. Whatever your vocation, your wages are scripturally, morally, and legally yours! You earn them. They are not a gift.

When you work hard, God's Law demands you receive your reward!

He that tilleth (works hard) his land shall have plenty
of bread:

Proverbs 28:19a

Child of God, if you are currently working hard, **expect** to receive your just reward.

Now there is another side to this law of reward!

No work = no reward.

God's Word is very emphatic about this.

> *But if any provide not for his own, and specially for those of his own house, he hath denied the faith, and is worse than an infidel.*
>
> *I Timothy 5:8*

Again, in II Thessalonians 3:10b:

> **If any would not work, neither should he eat.**

Plant this law firmly into your mind: like all of God's Spiritual Laws, it is an absolute! Those who "till" the land will have "plenty of bread." If your hard work is not bringing "plenty of bread" into your life right now, then some Spiritual Law of Poverty is working to stop God's desire for your life.

Day by day, as you examine the different Spiritual Laws for Prosperity, you will begin to understand that God's perfect will for your finances is for you to prosper and have more than enough.

REMEMBER:

- The laborer is worthy of his hire. (Luke 10:7b)
- Work hard and have plenty of bread. (Proverbs 28:19a)
- Those that won't provide for their own are worse than an infidel (non-believer). (I Timothy 5:8)
- If you won't work, God says you shouldn't eat. (2 Thessalonians 3:10)

Lesson 4: God's Law of Release

POVERTY IS NOT AN ACCIDENT, and neither is prosperity! Strict spiritual laws govern both.

The second "R" for poverty or prosperity is RELEASE.

The Spiritual Law of Release concerning prosperity says: **Be willing to release for the increase!**

> *There is (he) that scattereth, and yet increaseth; and there is (he) that withholdeth more than is fitting, but it tendeth to poverty.*
> *The liberal soul shall be made fat, and he that watereth shall be watered also himself.*
>
> *Proverbs 11:24,25*

Child of God, I do not know any other place in scripture where God makes it any clearer than here in Proverbs. Scatter your money, it will increase, and you will be prosperous. Hoard too much of it, more than is fitting, and you will be poor!

God's Spiritual Law will not change, no matter how uncomfortable it makes you feel. Right now, you may be saying:

"But Brother John, you mean I have to start giving my money away if I want to be prosperous? That doesn't make any sense."

You are right. In the eyes of the world it does not make sense. One of your "old" concepts, "set in concrete," says "Get all you can get, then keep the lid tight on the can." God's Spiritual Laws do not always make worldly sense, but they are His Truths, and will **always work**!

God's Spiritual Laws will not change: Release, and increase (prosper). Retain, and decrease (tend to poverty)!

REMEMBER:

- Prosperity is not an accident, and neither is poverty.
- Only when you DECIDE to put God's Spiritual Law of Release into action in your life can you expect God's promised Law of Increase to begin to operate for you too.
- God's Law of Receiving is clearly stated in Luke 6:38:

> *Give, and it shall be given unto you; good measure, pressed down, and shaken together, and running over, shall men give into your bosom. For with the same measure that ye measure it shall be measured to you again.*

Lesson 5: God's Law of Receiving

Remember the lame man at the gate called Beautiful? Acts 3:5 tells us that man was "expecting to receive something" from Peter and John when they brought him to his feet.

This man went away leaping and praising God!

How many times did Jesus himself walk by this man as he lay crippled at the gate? The man never expected to receive anything before. However, when Peter and John came by, the man was "expecting to receive something from them," and he was healed! The only different ingredient was his anticipation!

Child of God, those who are expecting to receive something are the ones who will receive it.

Most of God's Word is brought forth with an agricultural mentality: birds, fruit, planting, and harvest. Have you ever heard of a farmer who planted his precious seed and didn't expect a return?

Child of God, here is a shocker for you:

It is godly to give expecting to receive!

When God sent His Son, Jesus, to earth, the Father expected to receive something valuable in return: SONS AND DAUGHTERS!

God gave, expecting a desired result; He gave, expecting to receive.

And Jesus, our eternal role model, was willing to give **and** to receive.

Once, when Jesus visited a Pharisee's house, he allowed a woman to wash his feet with expensive ointment. When Simon criticized this woman, Jesus said, "Thou gavest me no water for my feet . . . but this woman hath anointed my feet with ointment," (Luke 7:44b,46b).

Jesus was a good receiver. Countless times in scripture we see Him receive food, lodging, gifts, and even a donkey. Jesus freely gave, but He also was willing to receive!

When you are not following in the footsteps of Jesus, or when you are not willing to be a good receiver, you will stop the abundant blessings God wants to flow into your life.

Your failure to expect to receive from others will result in a subconscious resistance to receiving. Many times pride keeps us from receiving, but Proverbs 16:18 gives us strong warning about pride:

> *Pride goeth before destruction, and an haughty spirit before a fall.*

Do not let your false pride harden your mind and stop you from receiving from God, or from others.

When Jesus said that it was more blessed to give than to receive, He didn't say we were not to receive.

Unless you begin to develop a receiving mentality, God cannot begin to bring prosperity into your life.

REMEMBER:

- God gives, EXPECTING TO RECEIVE. He gave Jesus, expecting to receive you as a spiritual son or daughter.
- Jesus was a good receiver.
- Pride and a "hardened" mind will restrict and slow God's prosperity into your life.

Lesson 6: God's Law of Sowing

When a farmer puts a seed into the ground, he does not get back just one seed. When he puts that seed into the earth, a divinely ordered process begins. The seed produces a stalk of corn, the stalk produces several ears of corn, and each ear produces hundreds of new seeds . . .

ALL FROM THE ONE SEED THE FARMER PLANTED!

But, Child of God, notice a very important point: the farmer had to **SOW THE SEED** first before there could be a harvest. And, the more seed he sows, the larger the harvest will be.

Remember 2 Corinthians 9: 6,7a and 10 from The Living Bible:

But remember this — if you give little, you will get little.

A farmer who plants just a few seeds will get only a small crop, *but* ***if he plants much, he will reap much.***

Every one must make up his own mind as to how much he should give.

For God, who gives seed to the farmer to plant, and later on, good crops to harvest and eat, ***will give you more and more seed*** *to plant, and will make it grow so that you can give away more and more fruit from your harvest.*

Every day you make a choice either to sow some of your seed, or to eat it. When you exercise faith and sow some of your seed, you release God's Laws of Prosperity. When you give in to your fears, and eat your seed, or hide it, you release God's Laws of Poverty.

Do not let your circumstances rule you.

They may tell you that "you can't afford to sow anything into the Gospel now." But Scripture clearly tells us that if we are ruled by our circumstances, we won't ever sow.

He that observeth the wind shall not sow; and he that regardeth the clouds shall not reap.

Ecclesiastes 11: 4

If you do not sow, you cannot reap, but God's word clearly tells you to sow in **all circumstances**!

In the morning sow thy seed, and in the evening ***withhold not thine hand;*** *for thou knowest not whether shall prosper, either this or that, or whether they both shall be alike good.*

Ecclesiastes 11:6

REMEMBER:

- Sow seed, and you will prosper. (2 Corinthians 9:6)
- When you sow, do not look to your circumstances. (Ecclesiastes 11:4)
- Sow regularly to every good work. (Ecclesiastes 11:6)

Lesson 7: God's Law of Reaping

Child of God, the following statement is so simple it is deceptive. In actual practice, most saints do not believe it. If they did, they would all be enjoying God's Prosperity in their lives:

IF YOU SOW, YOU WILL REAP!

Say this statement aloud several times. Let it sink into your spirit: **"If I sow, I will reap."**

This is God's law; it cannot and will not fail!

God warns us not to be fooled or deceived.

> Let him that is taught in the word (share with) him that teacheth in all good things. **Be not deceived; God is not mocked: for whatsoever a man soweth, that shall he also reap.**
>
> For he that soweth to his flesh shall of the flesh reap corruption; but he that soweth to the Spirit shall of the Spirit reap life everlasting.
>
> And let us not be weary in well doing; **for in due season we shall reap, if we faint not.**
>
> Galatians 6:6-9

God's Spiritual Law of Prosperity says:

1. Sow the seed.
2. In due season, reap the harvest.
3. What you sow is what you will harvest.

As you sow your seeds into the Gospel of Jesus Christ, you will reap His harvest! God will take your seed and MULTIPLY IT BACK to you.

Also notice the timing of the harvest. When will we reap? "In due season."

So do not sow your seed one day, and expect to reap a harvest the next morning. Would a farmer plant his crops on Thursday, and then on Friday take his combine out into the field waiting for the corn to appear?

28

Here's the final, vital point.

You will reap what you sow: "Whatsoever a man soweth, that shall he also reap." If you sow apples, you will reap apples. If you sow corn, you will reap corn. If you sow love, you will reap love. And, if you sow money, you will reap money.

Do not sow "good deeds," and expect God to return finances to you. Good deeds sown will bring back a harvest of good deeds!

His Spiritual Law says if you sow good deeds, you will reap good deeds, not finances. If you desire more wealth and more money to meet your needs, then put more money into God's Kingdom. You must first sow money in order to reap a money harvest.

Even unsaved farmers know this, while many of the sons of God do not.

REMEMBER:

- Unsaved farmers know that if they sow, they will reap.
- Unsaved farmers know they can reap only the kind they sow.
- Unsaved farmers know you do not reap in the same season you sow.

Do you see now how important it is to know God's Laws of the Harvest?

POVERTY OR PROSPERITY?
IN SUMMARY

Can you feel your mind struggling to hang onto the old, comfortable concepts as you read this book each day? The startling statements in God's Word often shock and shake our old standard Christian concepts about poverty and prosperity.

Child of God, recognize your mind is now firmly engaged in the Biblical process of transformation – precept upon precept, line upon line, here a little, there a little. Now your mind is starting to challenge and weed out the unscriptural, unfounded concepts, and is replacing them with sound, Biblical truths. These truths will be able to set you free from want and insufficiency, and release God's abundance to you.

29

By now, I am sure you realize that this book, **FINANCING THE ENDTIME HARVEST—GOD'S WAY** will challenge and TRANSFORM YOUR THINKING in the area of God's abundant supply. Please continue to **PARTICIPATE IN THE PROCESS** as you read each day.

Do not try to find any quick, instant solutions in this book, but continue to use this proven Biblical method. Take one lesson per day, read it in the morning, and then read it again in the evening. Give the new thoughts and ideas from each lesson time to become embedded in your mind.

You are now on your way to breaking through your cycle of lack. You are on your way into the cycle of abundance and prosperity!

Just look at the startling progress you have already made in only the first seven lessons of your journey to a new prosperity mentality, and yet there are 83 even more powerful concepts that soon will be yours!

Now let's review the Biblical principles from this section which you are now making part of your new mind:

1. God gave you the POWER to get wealth! (Deuteronomy 8:18)

2. God wants you to prosper. (III John 2)

3. Hard workers will have plenty of bread. (Proverbs 28:19)

4. If you do not provide for your own, you are worse than a non-believer. (1 Timothy 5:8)

5. If you do not work, you will not eat. (2 Thessalonians 3:10)

6. Jesus was a giver, **and** a receiver. (Luke 7:44-46)

7. Sow much seed, and you will prosper. (2 Corinthians 9:6)

8. Do not look at your circumstances when you sow. (Ecclesiastes 11:4)

9. Sow all the time. (Ecclesiastes 11:6)

10. In due season, you will reap. (Galatians 6: 9)

Child of God, when God's Spiritual Laws for Prosperity begin to totally transform your mind, when your life come into absolute alignment with God's mind, then HIS abundant blessings will begin to flow into your life.

God says in Deuteronomy 28:8 (NKJ): "The Lord will command the blessing on you." He also says that the blessings will overtake you (in Deuteronomy 28:2). No matter how far from God's plan of abundance you are now, when you begin to comply with God's Spiritual Laws of Prosperity, He will overtake you with His blessings!

SECTION TWO:
HOW YOU CAN REAP IN
A RECESSION

Lesson 8: Reaping in recession

Recession, inflation, and economic hard times have been with mankind since virtually the beginning of time. They are not new conditions demanding new solutions. The Biblical answers to victoriously conquer these economic conditions first appear early in the book of Genesis.

And there was a famine in the land, beside the first famine that was in the days of Abraham.

Genesis 26:1a

God gave Isaac very specific instructions to follow in order to prosper during these economic hard times:

1. Stay faithful to God's commands.

The Lord told Isaac He would bless him because "Abraham obeyed my voice, and kept my charge, my commandments, my statutes, and my laws." (Genesis 26: 5)

Don't let circumstances ruin your good Christian habits and lifestyles. Many saints become inconsistent in times of economic pressure; fluctuation from your Christian principles will only weaken you further.

2. Don't follow the world's philosophy.

Because of the famine, everyone was leaving to go to Egypt, but the Lord had a different program for Isaac:

Go not down into Egypt; dwell in the land which I shall tell thee of:
Sojourn in this land, and I will be with thee, and will bless thee;

Genesis 26: 2b-3a

Do not move to a new location without God's command, not because of a rumor that there is prosperity in another city or state. Remember, God can bless you in **any** location.

Blessed shalt thou be in the city, and blessed shalt thou be in the field.

Deuteronomy 28:3

31

3. Sow generously during the famine.

Isaac went forth under the Lord's instructions, and he "sowed in that land, and received in the same year an hundredfold: and the Lord blessed him." (Genesis 26:12b)

Early on in God's precious Word He set down this principle of Biblical economics. God intended Isaac to conquer the famine, and gave him the prosperity principles to emerge victorious.

These same basic Biblical principles apply for you today. Begin to use them now in your own life.

REMEMBER:

- Stay faithful to God's commands.
- Don't follow the world's philosophy.
- Sow generously during the famine.

Lesson 9: The world's ways are not God's ways

If you want to prosper according to Biblical principles, you must first forget most of the world's notions and principles of prosperity.

When everyone around Isaac was heading for Egypt, God told him to stay put – to ignore the world's answer to the famine problem – and sow in the midst of the famine! (For complete details, see the 26th chapter of Genesis.)

The world's answer was to flee.

The **Word's answer** was to stay and sow.

Ecclesiastes 11:4 clearly shows how the world's way is different from God's way when dealing with economic matters:

He that observeth the wind shall not sow; and he that regardeth the clouds shall not reap.

The people who were fleeing to Egypt in Isaac's day were looking too closely at their unpleasant circumstances. They observed the winds of hard times. They regarded the clouds of gloom and doom.

So, they uprooted their families, abandoned their possessions and their homes, and headed straight for Egypt. After all, everybody was doing it, but it was sowing, not fleeing, that delivered Isaac from his circumstances; the seeds he sowed delivered him.

God told Isaac to stay and sow the seeds for a harvest in the midst of a famine. He said,

"Isaac, don't look at your circumstances. Don't look at the famine around you. Ignore the winds and the clouds, and focus only on your desired goal—the need to eat and to prosper. If you want food for your family in the midst of famine, then you must first sow the seeds that will produce the harvest." So Isaac sowed the seeds, and God produced a harvest, without following the world's methods.

Do not listen to the world's answers, even when the winds of hard times hit your family or the clouds of gloom and doom are all around you. Instead, seek the voice of God.

His way is not the world's way.

The world says to hoard all you can in the midst of a famine. The Word of God says to plant seed, and expect to reap a harvest.

REMEMBER:

Hard times are the wrong times to stop giving to God.

Lesson 10: If you want more money

Right now you may find yourself in a situation similar to Isaac. He was in the midst of a harsh famine, and you may be in the midst of your own harsh, economic famine.

If you live in North America, your family is probably getting enough basic foods to eat, but your "prosperity" seems to stop right there. Your paycheck just never seems to stretch far enough to pay the rent, the utilities, and all your other obligations.

Your stomach may be full—but your pockets are empty!

So what do you do now?

Do what Isaac did:

Refuse to become fearful because of your circumstances. Remember if you do not ignore the winds and the clouds, and do not follow God's biblical principles, you will not reap a harvest.

> *He that observeth the wind shall not sow; and he that regardeth the clouds shall not reap.*
>
> *Ecclesiastes 11:4*

In the midst of an economic famine, the world tells you to hoard your money, to watch it very closely, and not spend one dime that isn't absolutely necessary.

Yes hard times are a time for priority only spending; foolish waste in hard times is not godly wisdom. But, whatever you do, don't count God out of your priority giving. Remember, giving to Him is your way out of the crisis.

33

The world's philosophy in hard times is to hoard the little corn they have left; then they starve in the process.

Christians should always remember that some financial seeds are for eating, and some are for planting so you can have a much needed financial harvest.

If you desire more money in the midst of an economic famine, then you must begin to sow more "money seeds" that will reap you a greater money harvest! Without sowing seeds, there can be no harvest. Simply stated, you must start giving more to God so that He can release more finances to you.

Whatever you do, don't feel like you are the only one with financial problems. Everyone experiences hard economic situations from time to time. But, child of God, don't make the fatal mistake of tightening up with God when things get tight!

Remember Isaac. He was one of God's children, and he obeyed God's laws. He planted good valuable seed in a time when everyone else was hoarding seeds, and his seed came up – even in the midst of a famine! Why? It's because he planted in accordance with God's command.

If you want more money in your hands each month, then plant more "money seeds" into the Gospel each month. When a child of God plants money seeds, you have God's word that a money harvest will come up, even in the midst of your worst economic famine.

Lesson 11: Give away what you lack

In the last few lessons, you have learned how God wants us to deal with famine. You saw how Isaac survived the famine through his obedience to God and his willingness to plant precious seed in the midst of famine. When you are in the midst of an economic famine, it is important that you . . .

   – **DO NOT EAT TOO MUCH OF THE SEED CORN.**

Some should be eaten, but some must be planted!

Look at how God rewarded the widow at Zarephath for her willingness to obey God and follow His principles of Biblical economics. (You will find the complete details in 1 Kings 17: 8- 16.)

The little widow was nearly out of food. She had only enough for one final meal. When Elijah asked her for "a morsel of bread," she replied:

"I have not a cake, but (only) an handful of meal in a

barrel, . . . that I may go in and (prepare) it for me
and my son, that we may eat it, and die."

1 Kings 17: 12b

Child of God, this little widow was experiencing her own personal famine. She was down to her last meal! But Elijah exhorted her to share her last cake with him (Elijah represented God, much in the same way churches and ministries do today). He promised if she obeyed, then:

The barrel of meal shall not waste (be used up), . . .
until the day that the Lord sendeth rain upon the
earth.

1 Kings: 17:14b

The turning point was when she actually gave the food away. The world would have told this little widow that it was sensible to hoard her small bit of remaining meal, to keep what little she had for her and her son before they die.

But, God works by different principles. She was exhorted to share her meal with God's minister, and then let God provide the harvest. She literally planted seed in the darkest part of the famine, because Elijah convinced her that if she planted seeds, she would reap a harvest.

So the little widow obeyed, and met the need of the man of God. As a result of her willingness to plant seeds, and her refusal to observe the winds and clouds of famine, God miraculously met her need.

The barrel of meal (was not used up), neither did the
cruse of oil fail, according to the word of the Lord,
which he spake by Elijah.

I Kings 17: 16

REMEMBER:

The golden rule works with God as well as with man. What you want done for yourself, you must first do for others. When you help the need of God and His workers, He will meet your needs.

Whatever you want men to do to you, do also to them.

Matthew 7:12a NKJ

Lesson 12: Plant in good ground

Simply sowing seed is not enough to reap a harvest; you must be very careful **where** you sow. If you throw all your seed onto a concrete slab, you will not reap a harvest.

One key principle of biblical economics is that you must **always sow your seeds in good ground**.

Remember, the best and most fertile ground in which you can plant your seed is the ground consecrated and dedicated to producing a harvest for the sons and daughters of God. Don't let sentimentalism or denominational allegiances sway you away from the best ground in which to plant your seed.

When times are financially difficult, you can reap your most abundant harvest by planting your precious seeds into God's proven, producing works.

YOUR ECONOMIC CIRCUMSTANCES ESTABLISH THE VALUE OF THE SEEDS YOU PLANT!

The money seeds of God's children are the most precious when they are scarce. When your money seeds to put into God's work are very scarce, take comfort and let your faith grow by what God says about your precious seeds:

> He that goeth forth and weepeth, **bearing precious seed**, shall doubtless come again with rejoicing, bringing his sheaves with him.
>
> *Psalms 126:6*

Now that should give you comfort and boldness to give to God's work even in tight financial times. God absolutely guarantees precious seed will bring back a return; His Word says they "shall **doubtless** come again with rejoicing."

Your precious seed has a guarantee of success and harvest!

God's Word abounds with BIBLICAL KEYS that will open the very treasure house of God for you. One of these keys, and perhaps the most vital of all, is that you must plant your seeds in good fertile ground to reap the best harvest. Very carefully pick the ministries you invest in – those Christ-honoring, soul-winning, Word-centered ministries who properly manage the money they are given.

Don't forget, when the dark clouds of hard times come into your life, God's Word can guide you out of your difficulty and into good times. Always remember that following God's direction in your giving won't get you into trouble, but it will get you out. God knows how much you give, and how much of the precious seed you have left. So, when your finances get tight, don't stop giving! Plant your precious seeds very carefully on good ground, and God will return an abundant harvest to you.

36

Lesson 13: Nothing is "luck" with God

The principles God established in His Word to guide you are absolute. They are not subject to luck. The widow at Zarephath gave from her scarce food supply, and she received her food supply back from God.

It was not luck – it was a direct application of God's Law of Increase. The widow **gave** from her precious meal, and God **returned** an abundance of precious meal to her, in fulfillment of the divine principle found in God's Word:

> For with the same measure that ye (measure), it shall
> be measured to you again.
>
> Luke 6: 38

I cannot emphasize this enough. The widow did not run into a streak of good luck. She obeyed God, and gave from her precious seed. God **honored His Word** by bestowing His abundant blessings on her! God, seeing her meager circumstances, realized that she had given in a very great measure. He knew that this woman's gift to His servant was a great sacrificial measure – it was her last cake, and all that stood between her and starvation – and God's Word says she received back a very large measure from God: an unending supply of meal and oil!

In Luke 21, Scripture tells of another poor widow who gave her precious seed. Jesus saw her give two mites, a large sum of money for a poor widow; it was all she had. Jesus honored this widow when he said:

> Of a truth I say unto you, that this poor widow hath
> cast in more than they all:
> For all these have of their abundance cast in unto the
> offerings of God: but she of her penury (poverty or
> need) hath cast in all the living that she had.
>
> Luke 21: 3b-4

Jesus not only saw into her pocketbook, but He saw into her heart! Her "measure" without a doubt was greater than any rich man in the temple: she gave "all the living that she had" with a heart of expectation and love.

Child of God, are you starting to grasp the spiritual principles in these examples? The two widows did not run into a streak of luck; they actually set in motion a principle of Biblical economics: they loosed the superior spiritual principles of God to work in the midst of their circumstances. They literally left the realm of chance and committed their future well-being to God's promises instead of the whims of economic circumstances.

Maybe right now you are like these widows: your money supply is scarce, and your gift to the gospel will come only from "precious seed." You have a choice. You can hoard your seed, **or** you can do like the widows did, and give out of your scarcity.

When you give, know that you are not subject to the whimsical fate of luck; instead, you are anchoring your future to God's superior principles of biblical economics. The Heavenly Father will honor your faith. Scripture shows that when we measure our best to God, He measures His best to us.

Leave the realm of fate and enter the realm of faith.

Lesson 14: How to start reaping NOW!

If you want to start reaping financial blessings in your life right now, you must follow the principles God has given us in Scripture.

Isaac sowed his seed in famine, when everyone around him was hoarding their seed and fleeing to Egypt.

The widow at Zarephath fed the man of God from her last bit of meal; she provided him with a cake made literally from the "bottom of the barrel."

The poor widow at the temple gave "all of the living she had" in the offering.

In all three cases, these desperate people STARTED TO REAP by following three basic principles:

1. They started right where they were at the point of their need.

2. They all planted precious seeds, despite their circumstances. Each refused to observe the winds and clouds of gloom and doom.

3. All planted out of their lack, their need. They gave their precious seeds in extremely hard times, and all three received God's abundant blessing in their lives in the midst of hard times.

Child of God, the same spiritual principles which allowed Isaac and the two widows to start reaping, will work for you too!

If you want to start reaping, then start sowing your precious seed into the Gospel, and it will return back to you!

They that sow in tears (hard times) shall reap in joy.
He that goeth forth and weepeth, bearing precious
seed (the last seed from the "bottom of the barrel"),

shall doubtless *come again with rejoicing, bringing his sheaves with him.*

Psalms 126: 5-6

Notice God's promise to you: When you sow precious seed, you **SHALL DOUBTLESS** rejoice when you receive the harvest from your seed-sowing!

This is not a matter of luck.

This is not a matter of hard work (although God honors hard work too).

This **is** a matter of obedience: when you are obedient to God's Word, God will honor His Word to accomplish the promise He made.

It is a matter of law – God's Law: laws we must always obey, and which God will not deny.

HOW YOU CAN REAP IN RECESSION

IN SUMMARY

Child of God, you should be experiencing the Biblical process of mind transformation as you study these lessons.

Remember, I told you God's way to change your mind is precept upon precept, line upon line, here a little, there a little.

With each new lesson and precept, your mind is filtering out the mistaken ideas that are polluting the precious living waters of God's Word in your mind.

With each new biblical concept you accept from God's Word, you are displacing an old, destructive concept from your mind; you are becoming closer and closer to what God would have you become!

For years, the devil has told you most people are prosperous because they are lucky. Hopefully that old worldly concept is now being rooted out of your mind, and is now being replaced with God's sound Biblical concept:

When you sow precious seed, you will doubtless reap a harvest. It has nothing at all to do with luck – it is according to a principle of biblical economics.

The devil has told you for years that when you experience tight financial times, you must hold onto every penny you have, and slow down your giving to God.

Hopefully that old erroneous concept is now gone from your mind, and you have replaced it with the biblical principle which guarantees we will receive a harvest – rejoicing – when we plant our precious seed!

Isaac sowed in hard times, and reaped in good measure!

The two widows sowed in hard times, and reaped in good measure!

And now, if you too will sow in hard times, surely you will reap in good measure!

PARTICIPATE IN THIS PROVEN PROCESS!

Continue to read one lesson in the morning, and reread it again in the evening. Allow the new thoughts and ideas from each page to transform your mind.

Remember, Satan wants you in financial bondage – in a constant unbroken cycle of lack. He knows that as long as you are always struggling to pay the bills, you cannot give the much-needed funds you desire to give to God's great endtime harvest.

Satan also knows that when you begin to grasp **AND APPLY** these biblical principles in your life, you will have the abundance you need to give to every good ministry God lays on your heart.

Yes, even Satan knows that if you apply these biblical principles, you will reap a mighty blessing, and will want to be a good steward of the riches God **WILL DOUBTLESS** bring into your life.

Do not be deceived. These new concepts – these new Biblical principles – are of absolutely no value to you **until** you start to step out in faith and apply them in your daily living. Nothing will happen until you put these principles into practice.

So begin today.

Give. Give what you need, remembering that "whatsoever a man soweth, that shall he also reap." (Galatians 6:7b)

Give to the Gospel.

Plant your precious seeds in fertile ground, and watch God unfold a financial miracle in your life!

SECTION THREE:
GOD — THE GREATEST GIVER!

Lesson 15: God freely gives *all things*

God has always been a great gift giver!

For by grace are ye saved through faith; and that not of yourselves: **it is the gift of God***: Not of works, lest any man should boast.*

Ephesians 2: 8-9

You see, it is God's nature to give; **God, the Father, freely gives us all things!** Our very salvation is a free gift from God.

He that spared not his own Son, but delivered him up for us all, how shall he not with him also **freely give us all things***?*

Romans 8: 32

Notice that God wants to give us "all things"—not just those things that are spiritual, or heavenly, but "all things!" That includes money for food, clothes, rent, gas, and even something left over for entertainment.

All things.

If God did not withhold His own Son (nothing was more precious than His own Son, Jesus), then it is not difficult to understand that God will give us ALL things. If we can focus on the greatest Gift, Jesus Christ—and that gift has already been given—then no lands, houses, treasures, or needs of any kind will be withheld from us.

Even the Holy Ghost is freely given to all that ask. If ye then, being evil, know how to give good gifts unto your children, how much more shall your heavenly Father **give the Holy Spirit** to them that ask him?

Child of God, let this concept sink into your spirit. Our God is a giving God! He desires to give us "all things."

According as his divine power hath **given unto us all things** *that pertain unto life and godliness,*

II Peter 1:3a

God is the Supreme Giver of the universe. He gives to us according to His divine power! He desires that we have ALL THINGS that pertain to life and godliness. Get that into your spirit and force out any thoughts that do not come into conformity with this promise from God!

41

Lesson 16: God wants YOU to be like Him!

Man is created in the image of God, but Satan changed that when mankind fell into sin. But those who accept Jesus Christ are restored and brought into the image of God once again. Yes, God wants you to be like Him! He literally envisions you like Himself:

As he (Jesus) is, so are we in this world.

I John 4: 17b

You know that God is a giver.
You know that Jesus is a giver.
And, you know that the Holy Spirit is a giver.
Now, it is important for you to understand that God wants YOU to be a giver! Jesus constantly urged His disciples to give:

1. He told them to give to all that ask.
2. He told them that freely they received, and freely they should give.
3. He urged His disciples to give the people food to eat.
4. Jesus taught, "Give, and it shall be given unto you."
5. Jesus urged us to give to the poor.

Child of God, Jesus lived a lifestyle of giving. He said:
I am come that they might have life, and that they might have it more abundantly.

John 10:10

Yes, God wants you to be like His Son, Jesus – not just in a future life when we will be like Him, but right now, by imitating Him.

You can start by taking ahold of His wonderful characteristic of giving: begin to see yourself as a great giver too. The giving of Jesus Christ went into every realm: when he met the depressed, HE GAVE them a light heart. When he met the hungry, HE GAVE them food to eat. When he encountered the naked, HE GAVE them clothes to wear.

Jesus GAVE and GAVE and GAVE and GAVE.

Ultimately, HE GAVE the final ultimate sacrifice – his life, so we could have **eternal** life!

You may never be called upon to give your life's blood for another person, but starting today, you can literally become a giver of every good thing that those around you need.

Remember that with each act of giving, you will receive, so that one day, if you continue in faithful giving, you will have enough to give in every way God desires.

Remember, you are becoming like Him, not all at once, but step-by-step, progressively, from glory to glory.

Lesson 17: Give joyfully. Reap abundantly.

God freely gives His gifts to us. Our salvation comes to us freely. The Holy Spirit is given freely. And the gifts of the Spirit are given freely.

God expects the same willingness to give freely from us:

> *So let him give; not grudgingly, or of necessity: for* **God loveth a cheerful giver**.
>
> *2 Corinthians 9: 7b*

The next time you write out a check to your local church or favorite ministry, remember that the Lord desires you to give with a "cheerful" heart. Sing a sacred song as you write out that check. Think of the joy your money will bring to the lives of those who will be saved or delivered through it. Put a big smile on your face when your drop your next offering into the collection basket.

As you give with your cheerful heart, remember you must also give abundantly if you want to reap abundantly:

> *But this I say, He which soweth sparingly shall reap also sparingly; and he which soweth bountifully shall reap also bountifully.*
>
> *2 Corinthians 9:6*

At first this scripture may seem a bit unfair. You could easily be thinking: "But Brother John, I don't have a lot to give. I have only a small amount of money each week that I can give to God's work. I quess that means I will reap sparingly."

Child of God, that is not true!

Remember the poor widow with the two mites? Jesus said she gave **more** than all the other rich men in the temple. Why? Her giving, in proportion to her income, was a much greater sacrifice than anyone else made! Jesus saw her heart. The poor widow gave "bountifully," and God rewarded her bountifully. Remember, "with the same measure" you give, God will give back to you again.

When you give "bountifully" from your own supply of money, remember, it is the **proportion** of the whole amount that you give, not the amount which determines if your gift is bountiful – and give with a "cheerful heart": God will abundantly bless you.

So do not be discouraged if your offerings to God are not as much as you want them to be. God looks at your offerings in relation to how much you have left after you give.

43

Lesson 18: Giving ALWAYS results in receiving

Memorize the title of today's study. It is a vital principle of Biblical economics:

GIVING ALWAYS RESULTS IN RECEIVING!

No exceptions. You have God's Word on it.

Give, and it shall be given unto you; **good measure,** **pressed down,** *and* **shaken together,** *and* **running over,** *shall men give into your bosom. For with the same measure that ye (measure) it shall be measured to you* **again.**

Luke 6: 38

Look closely at these KEY POINTS:

1. God promises to return your gift to you. He says YOU WILL RECEIVE a "good measure," literally "running over." God will abundantly bless you when you give to Him.

2. God says your blessings will come from "men" who shall give "into your bosom." God uses men, and so He has no difficulty blessing you from **unexpected** places. The source God uses isn't important; what is vital is that you understand the Biblical principle – when you give, you will receive back again for giving.

3. By the same measure you give, you will receive. Remember, the "measure" is not **how much** you give, but how much you give **IN PROPORTION to your income**. This scripture does not promise if you give $5, you will receive back $5. It says if you give $5, and that $5 is simply casual pocket money, you will not receive a very big "measure" back. You will receive the $5 back, but not in a greatly multiplied measure.

But, if that $5 is a very critical part of your remaining funds, a precious seed out of your limited remaining seed – it becomes a "great measure" in God's eyes, and you will receive a "great measure" in return from Him; it will be greatly multiplied.

When you become a giver, you automatically move yourself into the realm of a receiver. There are no exceptions to this. However, there are levels of receiving: "some thirty, and some sixty, and some an (hundredfold)." (Mark 4:8b) The measure you use in giving will establish the measure that is applied to you in receiving, no matter with what measure you give, when you give to God, you will receive back.

Give, and it shall be given unto you.

Luke 6:38a

REMEMBER:
> *Be not deceived (don't be fooled), God is not mocked (He cannot be fooled): for whatsoever a man soweth, that shall he also reap.*
>
> *Galatians 6:7*

Now you understand why the title of this lesson is so important. Do not forget it! Giving always results in receiving.

Lesson 19: Giving is your God-given right

> *Give, and it shall be given unto you; good measure, pressed down, and shaken together, and running over, shall men give into your bosom. For with the same measure that ye (measure) it shall be measured to you again.*
>
> *Luke 6:38*

These promises are not restricted to any particular group of saints; it is every saint's right to claim these promises, if they put God's principle of giving to work.

Day by day your mind is being transformed, line upon line, and precept upon precept, until you fully understand what a joy and a God-given right it is for you to be a giver.

Imagine if your local bank promised every time your wrote a check, they would give you "more than enough" money to cover the draft. Surely you would consider yourself a very fortunate person.

At first, you would probably be a bit cautious, and write checks for moderate amounts. But, as the bank proved itself faithful and honored your checks again and again, and put more money in your account, you would soon realize this wonderful new relationship was opening a whole new life to you and your loved ones. Not only would it be a blessing to you, but any neighbor or friend who found out about your bank would want the "right" to the same sort of account. It would be wrong for your bank to offer this program to only you.

Of course we know banks don't operate this way, but God clearly declares that He does!

He promises to give us back more than we give, and He guarantees this to **all** His depositors (those who give to His work). When I say "ALL," I mean ALL! God says in His Word that He is no respecter of persons.

More than once He promises we will receive back MORE THAN WE GIVE, every single time!

45

Are you grasping that? Since the entire resources of the universe are at His creative disposal, our Heavenly Father will never run out of funds, so He will always be able to meet his promises of giving back to us more than we give to Him.

Child of God, do you see what this is doing to your thinking on giving to God? Giving to Him is not an obligation – it is AN OPPORTUNITY to put God's Biblical principles into action! It is literally operating your heavenly checking account according to a principle that contradicts the world: **the more you give away to God's work, the more He will return to you so you can give to His work again!**

Yes, God will give you much so that you can give away much,

2 Corinthians 9:11a
TLB

If the entire Body of Christ began to operate in this Biblical principle, we would witness the abundance Moses experienced in Exodus 36: 6b. His people were so willing to give to build the sanctuary that Moses finally had to stop the giving.

*Let neither man nor woman make any more work for the offering of the sanctuary. So the people were restrained from bringing. For the stuff they had was sufficient for all the work to make it, and **too much**.*

Child of God, begin to grasp your God-given right of giving and God's obligation to return to you more than you gave, then there will come a day when the abundance of God will literally overtake you and every desire you have in giving to God will be possible, with plenty left over to meet your every need and want.

Lesson 20: God's will for YOU — more than enough

When you give to God, your gift allows God the opportunity to bless you, to keep His Promises, and to give you more than enough. By your faithful obedience in giving your tithes and offerings, you set God's Biblical principles of economics into motion.

Your precious gifts unleash God's power in several areas of your life:

1. Your gift will prosper you. God promises that when you are a giver, "whithersoever it turneth, it prospereth." (Proverbs 17: 8b)

2. Your gift provides you with a place in life, and will bring you before "great" (godly) men in our society:

> *A man's gift maketh room for him, and bringeth*
> *him before great men.*
>
> *Proverbs 18: 16*

3. Your gift will even bring you friends:

> *Every man is a friend to him that giveth gifts.*
>
> *Proverbs 19:6 b*

This does not advocate buying friends with your money. It simply sets up a magnetism that draws others to you.

4. Your gift will stop anger that is focused against you:

> *A gift in secret pacifieth anger:*
>
> *Proverbs 21:14a*

Just for fun, try this when someone is angry with you: send them a secret gift and watch their anger quieten. Don't ask me how it works, but it does, for I have seen it happen again and again.

Child of God, do you understand what God intends to do to your life when you give?

When you are a cheerful giver, God will bless you and give back many blessings to you – out of His abundance! He wants you to prosper, to have a place in life, to mingle with "great" (godly) men, to have friends, instead of enemies.

God cares about YOU, and He ministers to you in many areas when you unleash the Biblical process of giving. Not only does He minister to you in the area of finances, but He also ministers to you spiritually, and to those around you. Being a great giver releases a positive, cooperative atmosphere all around you!

Lesson 21: Giving will spread the Gospel

In lesson 19, you read how Moses was overwhelmed by the generosity of the Israelites and asked them to stop giving! They had literally given too much!

I believe if enough Christians grasp the principles of Biblical economics in this book, and then apply them in their daily lives, every church, every mission outreach, every Christian television ministry, and yes, every Christian home in our world will scream, "Stop, Lord, we've got **too much!**"

47

Your faithfulness in giving to God's work guarantees that a day of abundant prosperity will eventually come to you when the reapers will literally overtake the sowers. But no matter how long it takes the whole church world, you can start right now to have more than enough by applying these principles and seeing their benefits materialize in your life right now.

That is not **my** promise, it is **God's promise**!

When you catch this vision, you can without fear – ask God how much your special financial gift should be to a certain Christian television ministry, a strong missionary outreach, or to your own local church. Whatever God tells you to do, you will have the money to do it – when you catch this God-given vision!

Remember, giving is a KEY part of your Christian walk. It is not a separate, non-spiritual act of writing out a check; giving of your finances to God is a deep, personal interaction with God Himself, and is as much a part of your Christianity as your time of prayer.

So do not just give your money without thought, or without prayer. Ask God where you should direct your gifts, and even ask Him **how much** you should give. God has a definite plan for your finances, and He cares about your individual offerings.

Nearly 20 percent of all the verses in the Bible relate to finances, land, money, goods, cattle, personal belongings, etc.– in various forms, so you can be sure God is concerned about your personal finances.

He cares about every part of your life, and each part relates to your overall walk as a Christian.

Remember, God is a great giver, and He wants you to be one too:

> *How then shall they call on him in whom they have not believed? and how shall they believe in him of whom they have not heard? and how shall they hear without a preacher?*
> *And how shall they preach, except they be sent?*
> *Romans 10: 14-15a*

I believe there is one answer to this marvelous passage: they will be sent by those who put God's plan of giving and receiving to work until they have complete dominion over every aspect of their finances!

GOD – THE GREATEST GIVER
IN SUMMARY

Giving started with God. He set the example, He demonstrated how to give, and He has determined the rewards of giving.

If you are uncomfortable with any of the concepts you have learned in the past few lessons, don't argue with me! These are not Brother John's ideas, they are God's!

Brother John did not determine you should give away what you lack – **God did**.

Brother John did not determine that you reap what you sow – **God did**.

Brother John did not decide to tell you "if you give, you will get a bunch of nice things back," – **That's God's idea**.

If this bothers you, talk to God about it – it's His idea, not mine!

Why are some of us so set in our old ways of thinking that we simply label something as "untrue" when it does not agree with our preconceived concepts?

Child of God, truth aligns with God's concepts, not with our own ideas. Whether we agree or not, God will prosper those who give to His work! God will bless those who give, and He will bless them in proportion to the "measure" that they give. Those that give sacrificially will receive a greater portion back from God than those who give out of their abundance. You see, God knows the difference in discretionary funds and non-discretionary funds; He cannot be fooled.

Remember, that's not my idea – it is God's!

All I am doing is reporting to you in context the verses of scripture many preachers ignore because of the controversy and turmoil they produce among the carnal minded "saints!"

So, you seldom hear verses that talk about God's desire for you to prosper, to have friends, to mingle with "great" (godly) men, to be successful, and have a position of respect among your peers.

These ideas likely are "new" to you, but they are not "new" to God; they have been around for eternity, and have been in the Bible since the very beginning.

These ideas did not come from a recent, revised edition of the Bible! They were not just uncovered on the Dead Sea scrolls. The verses you are reading have been in the Bible since it was first inspired by the Holy Ghost to the sacred writers.

Because the verses pertaining to the finances of the saints have not been properly applied over the past 2000 years, the

49

Church of God is now weak, anemic, under financed, and must literally beg each week for the funds to keep going, then spend those hard-earned tithes and offerings on mortgage payments while the world cries for spiritual ministry.

That's not what God intended.

Here is the challenge: If you will apply God's principles of Biblical economics in your own life, if you will muster the courage to unleash the process by giving—then your finances will be blessed abundantly, and the church of God will begin to grow beyond anything we can imagine.

Ministers will be trained and sent forth—because there will be "more than enough" money to send them.

Television programs will beam the Gospel around the world—because there will be "more than enough" money to buy the air time.

Churches will expand to hold the ever-increasing numbers of people attracted by the "new" Christians who always have "more than enough," even in the midst of "famine!"

This is exactly what John had in mind when he made his wonderful wish for us in 111 John 2:

> Beloved, I wish above all things that thou mayest prosper and be in health, even as thy soul prospereth.

Child of God, you have two choices:.

You can hold onto your old, traditional beliefs and continue to struggle from paycheck to paycheck.

Or you can APPLY God's economic principles in your own life, and cheerfully give in "good measure."

If every person reading this book chooses the second option, and begins to freely and joyfully give of their finances in "**good measure**," soon preachers and ministries all over the world will be screaming:

"Stop! Stop! We have enough! The endtime harvest is now assured."

And, God's people—His children—overwhelmed by God's love, will shout:

"Heavenly Father, you have given me a blessing so large I cannot contain it! Truly it is as the scriptures say: There is more than enough"!

SECTION FOUR:
10 TRUTHS ABOUT MONEY

Lesson 22: Finances are important!

If something is important to God, AND it has a very high priority on God's list of worthwhile subjects, don't you think it should be important to you?

By now, I pray it is firmly rooted into your spirit **that God does desire good things for you.** Not only does He want you to be spiritually strong and prosperous, but He also desires you to be prosperous in the material needs of your life and your family, such as food, clothing, housing, finances, and yes, even everything that pertains to the "good life."

God did not tell Isaac to forget about the famine and be spiritual. Instead, He told Isaac: 1. **where to live**, 2. **what to plant**, and 3. **what to expect** from his seeds. God wanted Isaac to have the material things necessary to live well **even in the midst of famine**!

You see, God **does care** about **your material needs**.

The Old and New Testament talk so much about "seeds" and "planting" because at the time they were written, the world was operating in an agricultural economy. Jesus simply related to the agricultural times in which He lived.

If Jesus were walking on the earth today, He would have a significant amount to say about home mortgages, trust deeds, government bonds, interest rates, mass production, and marketing trends – all of these would be liberally dispensed among the parables and similies he told.

Today it seems it is just fine for preachers to talk about religious matters, but somehow the topic of money and practical things are not spiritual, and should be left unsaid by God's men.

Nonsense. Money is to be a spiritual issue to the saints of God!

When the poor widow sacrificed her two mites in an offering in the temple, Jesus did not say: "Woman, your financial sacrifice does not matter to me. God is not interested in your money. All that matters to God is your spiritual needs – I'm not concerned about your material needs. Just learn how to grin and bear your financial condition."

Instead, Jesus praised her for her precious financial sacrifice. **Jesus knew the widow's heart!** Since the mites were a big part of her **necessary living expenses**, Jesus considered them a signifi-

51

cant gift – an **important** action! They were compared with the gifts of others – including very rich people – that day. Jesus even called over the disciples and made open comment about the faith of the widow as it was manifested in her money offering.

You see, money **is important to God.** Money is important to Jesus.

So, money **should be important to you**. In the next few weeks, let your mind and spirit grow into a deeper understanding of the **value of money – to you, to God, and to the spreading of the Gospel**.

Lesson 23: Money is not evil

One of the biggest mistakes I know about money comes from a misunderstanding of 1 Timothy 6:10a:

For the love of money is the root of all evil:

The mistake made here by the saints of God is in what they think the verse says. Read it carefully: "For **the love** of money is the root of all evil."

Now, many people do not read what the Bible really says. Instead, they read what **they want the Bible to say**. Please notice that this verse **does not say** money is evil! The verse clearly states that **the love of money** is at the root of all evil. Nothing at all is said about money itself in verse 10; all it says is that the love of money is at the root of all evil.

Yet, I've heard so many good Christians use this verse to justify their belief that God does not want them to have anything to do with money. They ignorantly believe that the Bible teaches that money is evil.

Child of God, this is a terrible mistake. God **does** want you to have money. God **does** care about your needs, and He knows that the lack of money can cause very serious problems in your life, as well as throughout society.

It doesn't take a genius to notice that people are holding up gas stations because they do not have money. All over the world, people are starving to death because they do not have money to buy food. People are freezing because they do not have enough money to buy the proper fuel to heat their homes. People with poor health could be well if they had the money to buy the proper foods.

The Bible even says "Money answereth all things." (Ecclesiastes 10:19) Money itself is neither good or evil. It only has the ability to do what its owner wants to do. The owner is in charge. The money is neither good or bad; it is whatever its owner is. It serves him **without question**; it is ready to do good or evil at its **owner's discretion**.

My money is good money. The only way for money to do any evil thing is for it to come under the control of an evil person. The Bible tells me that if I believe in the Lord Jesus Christ, and live after the precepts He has taught me, then I am a good man. And when I spend my money, I spend it for good things.

My money is spent on spreading the Gospel of Jesus Christ, on my family and their needs, and on helping others less fortunate than myself.

My money is not evil. The only way for money to do any evil is for it to come under the control of an evil person. Money simply manifests what is in its owner's heart. When the poor widow gave her two mites she showed Jesus she cared enough to give out of her want. Because she was a good woman, her money was "good money" and rather than loving it, she quickly and totally gave it into the offering in God's temple.

Luke 12: 34 says:
For where your treasure is, there will your heart be also.

If your heart is in line with God, then your treasure (your money) will literally be godly money. When your heart is right, you will put more and more of your money into the Gospel and less and less money into recreation and frivolous diversions.

Mark this truth: **money is not evil**. It is a magnificent tool in the hands of godly men and women to help bring the saving message of Jesus Christ to lost souls around the world! Stretch your faith to see that God wants you to have as much money as you have the faith to use properly.

REMEMBER:

God will give you much so that you can give away much.

2 Corinthians 9:11a TLB

Lesson 24: Improper attitudes towards money *can* harm you

When talking about money, like any other topic in scripture, it is important to maintain a balance. In the last lesson we determined that money is not evil. Today, I want to plant in your thinking the proper balance on this controversial topic: Money **can** harm you, because it is very powerful.

Money does have the potential to harm you if you do not control it in accordance with God's specific instructions. It can harm you, for example, if you use it for dark and sinful purposes. It can harm you if you use it to buy destructive substances (drugs or narcotics). It can hurt you and others if you use it to fulfill the lusts of the flesh instead of the will of the Spirit.

In Matthew 19 Jesus tells the rich young ruler to sell all he has and to follow Him. When the young ruler could not give up his wealth, he proved that he was not in control of his riches, but instead his riches controlled him! Don't think for a moment that his money did not hurt him: it literally cost him his soul!

Money does have the potential to harm you if you cannot control it in accordance with God's will for your life! You are in real danger of your money hurting you whenever it begins to rule you, instead of **you ruling it**.

The "love of money" caused Judas Iscariot to betray Jesus. For just thirty pieces of silver, he handed Jesus over to be crucified, and lost his own soul.

When used improperly, or when given improper importance, money can **definitely** cause harm. Begin to view money like many other tools you have available for your use: how you use them determines whether they will do harm or do good.

Gasoline. Electricity. Guns. Cars. Explosives. Nuclear power. Airplanes. Money. All of these can improve the quality of man's life. And, all can cause **severe harm** when misused or out of control. Their blessing or harm to your life is determined by whether they are operated under your control or out of control.

Money can do many good things, but when money is not controlled by the Spirit of God in us, it can literally destroy us.

So don't be so naive as to think that money won't hurt you. It is very capable, if misused, of doing eternal damage.

Lesson 25: Money doesn't guarantee happiness

Many of the things which make us unhappy can be cured by money. For example, a father who is unhappy because he cannot provide food for his family will be happy when his paycheck comes.

But, money itself **never** guarantees happiness.

Think about this statement: If money guaranteed happiness, then all the rich folks would be marvelously happy, and all the poor folks would be miserably sad. You and I know that is not true. Rich people commit suicide. Rich people visit psychologists to treat their depression. Rich people deal with "unhappy" issues such as divorce, alcoholism, drug addiction, and yes, even financial problems. Many rich people spend the early part of their life **in misery** trying to accumulate their fortune, and then spend the latter part of their life **in misery** trying to hold onto the fortune they have accumulated.

Money simply does not guarantee happiness. True happiness and lasting peace will only come through a proper relationship with Jesus:

> *For the kingdom of God **is not food and drink**, but righteousness and peace and joy **in** the Holy Spirit.*
> *For he who serves Christ in these things is acceptable to God and approved by men.*
> *Therefore let us pursue the things which make for peace and the things by which one may edify another.*
> *Romans 14:17-19 NKJ*

When your relationship with God is right, your money will not cause you problems and unhappiness: instead, it will be a blessing and a source of happiness for you and others around you.

> *The blessing of the Lord, it maketh rich, and **he addeth no sorrow** with it.*
> *Proverbs 10:22*

God will not harm you by multiplying money back to you. When you have the right heart, and the right spirit in giving that money to Him, God will grant you riches. Although your God-given money will not guarantee you happiness, God does promise that the riches He gives you will not bring you sorrow.

You see, righteousness, peace, and joy are found in Him, **not** in money.

Lesson 26: People are not "destined" to be poor

Have you ever said to yourself: "I guess I'm just not meant to be rich. I must be destined to be poor, so I suppose it is time I accept my lot in life."

Many of the saints believe this. They believe God has somehow ordained a select few people to have all the wealth, and the rest to struggle in poverty all of their lives.

Notice the satanic deception in this statement. If you accept this lie, it immediately releases you from any responsibility for your financial circumstances, and places the blame for your insufficiency on God.

For God to determine some people are to be rich and some people are to be poor, is unfair, and is against God's divine nature, and His stated Word.

Instead, God has given to all of us STRICT SPIRITUAL LAWS which determine who receives wealth, and who remains poor. These laws for poverty and prosperity are clearly stated in God's Word, and are as absolute as the spiritual laws which govern your salvation.

The LAWS OF POVERTY say: If you are lazy and do not work, you will not receive provision. (See Proverbs 24:33,34)

The LAWS OF PROSPERITY say; If you are not lazy, if you will work without constant supervision, if you are liberal in your giving, and put Jesus first in your finances, then you will be prosperous. (See Proverbs 6:6-8, and Proverbs 11: 24,25)

God has given us these and other guidelines throughout scripture as His STRICT SPIRITUAL LAWS. When they are applied, they will determine the measure of prosperity or poverty you will experience in your own life.

If you are interested in winning the world to Christ, then it is important for you to understand these spiritual laws of prosperity.

Operating churches costs money.

Printing Bibles costs money.

Preaching the Word in foreign lands costs money.

Beaming godly television programs around the world costs money.

And, that money will come to the saints only when they begin to understand **and** apply God's Laws of Abundance in their lives.

God says that the good life is each saint's portion.

It is good and fitting for one to eat and to drink, and to enjoy the good of all his labor . . . for it is his (portion)

56

> *... Every man to whom God has given riches and wealth, and given him power to eat of it, to receive his (portion) and rejoice in his labor—this is the gift of God.*
>
> *Ecclesiastes 5:19 NKJ*

After reading this scripture, it is impossible to believe only a few are destined to wealth and the rest are destined to poverty. God has made **His plan** very clear in His Word!

Lesson 27: God wants YOU to be prosperous

Many Christians honestly believe poverty is godly. They think if a Christian is poor, he must really be in the center of God's will.

There are even misguided groups of people who believe that by taking "vows of poverty," they will somehow be more godly or more believable to those who hear them witness the Gospel. Many preachers have actually taught that if we have holes in our britches and no soles on our shoes, we are suffering for Jesus and making our testimony easier to believe!

Child of God, it is time for the saints to start believing God's Word, instead of their own ideas!

GOD'S WORD DOES NOT TEACH POVERTY!

I am going to share with you a scripture that is so shocking, and mind-shattering I recommend you read the entire passage several times and let the truth of this shocking Biblical concept begin to penetrate your spirit. It is without a doubt one of the greatest blows to the erroneous teaching that poverty enhances the testimony of the Gospel. (There is space here for only the final line. **See your Bible for the entire text.**)

> *Then said I, Wisdom is better than strength; nevertheless, **the poor man's wisdom is despised**, and **his words are not heard**.*
>
> *Ecclesiastes 9:16*

Don't let your traditional thinking close your mind and prevent you from seeing the real truth here: GOD WANTS YOU TO PROSPER.

If you do not prosper, **the world will not listen to your "wisdom"** when you share the Gospel. Sure, a few will listen to your testimony when you are poor, but many, many more will listen to your testimony when you are prospering!

We're talking about a miracle realm.

57

God wants to work a miracle beyond your miracle of salvation, beyond your miracle of the Holy Ghost, and even beyond your miracle of health; God wants to work the miracle of financial prosperity in your life, and set you up as one of His earthly stewards.

Remember 3 John 2:

Beloved, I wish above all things that thou mayest prosper and be in health, even as thy soul prospereth.

When opportunities come for you to give, then give. Even go beyond the opportunity. Be bold. Ask your pastor or your favorite television ministry, or your trusted ministry partner, what they need.

When you get ahold of this truth, you will experience such abundance you will need to find new opportunities to give. See in your spirit a whole new kind of relationship between the leaders of churches, ministries, and television outreaches.

Begin now to seed into God's work so He can begin to unleash His miracle of financial prosperity in your life. As God blesses you, your testimony will be a powerful witness for God. And, as people see that there is positive financial activity around you, they will seek your opinions, and give you the opportunity to freely and effectively witness to them about your God and His Son, Jesus Christ.

Lesson 28: You can increase your finances

By now, I hope you are beginning to understand that you are not an irreversible victim of your financial problems. You do not need to be held captive by the evil snares of poverty and insufficiency any longer.

There is nothing spiritual in poverty, nothing blessed in not being able to pay your bills, and nothing sacred about tattered clothes. God wants you to live in abundance, and He has given you specific instructions for increasing your finances.

Beloved, I wish above all things that thou mayest prosper and be in health, even as thy soul prospereth.

3 John 2

Child of God, this very day you can start on a Bible-centered plan to improve your financial condition. It will not be through luck. Not through inheritance. Not through a big breakthrough on an investment. But, by applying the spiritual laws of abundance

58

which God has given us to follow, you can start on the way to financial prosperity.

1. Give your gift to God cheerfully.

> . . . So let him give; not grudgingly, or of necessity: for God loveth a cheerful giver.
>
> 2 Corinthians 9:7b

Give your tithes and offerings (gifts over the tithe) with a cheerful heart.

2. Plant your seeds liberally.

We have already seen that when you sow sparingly, you will reap sparingly. But, when you sow bountifully, you shall reap bountifully.

> But remember this—if you give little, you will get little. A farmer who plants just a few seeds will get only a small crop, but if he plants much, he will reap much.
>
> 2 Corinthians 9:6 TLB

3. Strive to eliminate your debts as soon as possible.

> Owe no man any thing, but to love one another;
>
> Romans 13:8a

Set specific goals for getting out of debt and living on a cash basis.

4. Resist impulse buying.

Always seek God's will and guidance in your major purchases.

5. Invest wisely.

Wise counsel on your investment program is recommended. Listen only to qualified and reputable institutions—those who have a stable, long-term financial record, and are recommended by those you trust. Also, avoid "long shots" and "get rich quick" schemes.

However, do not fail to realize that throughout scripture, it is made very clear the best investment you can make to receive a steady and liberal steady return, and an ongoing increase in your finances

—is to invest in the spread of the Gospel!

Plant your money seeds liberally to take the message of salvation to a needy world, and God will see to it that you prosper NOW and in eternity:

> But he shall receive an hundredfold **NOW** in this time, . . . and in the world to come eternal life.
>
> Mark 10: 30

Remember, if you need an increase in your income, simply increase the measure of your giving:

> For with the same measure that ye (measure) it shall be measured to you again.
>
> Luke 6:38b

Lesson 29: God cares how much you give

If God didn't care how much or how often you gave, He would not have included so many instructions in Scripture concerning the methods, the time, and the attitudes for giving.

He repeatedly gives instructions about giving, including the specific day for giving:

> Upon the first day of the week let every one of you lay by him in store, as God hath prospered him,
>
> 1 Corinthians 16: 2a

God **does care when** you give, and **He cares how much** you give.

> But this I say, He which soweth sparingly shall reap also sparingly; and **he which soweth bountifully shall reap also bountifully.**
>
> 2 Corinthians 9:6

When Jesus walked on the earth, He watched the people giving their offerings in the temple:

> And Jesus sat (opposite) the treasury, and beheld how the people cast money into the treasury:
>
> Mark 12: 41a

Many Christians would prefer to have this scripture taken out of their Bible, but like it or not, it is there. Jesus sat and watched the people put their money into the offering.

And, as we have seen, Jesus was deeply moved by the attitude and the intentions of the giver. The poor widow who sacrificed her two mites was considered by Jesus to be the most generous giver in all the temple, because her gift was extremely large in proportion to her available money supply.

I want you to notice that Jesus was moved by the widow's giving. If we only tip God, we probably hope He doesn't notice, but when we get serious about giving and give a substantial portion of our income to the Lord, it is comforting to know that He takes notice and that proper giving is noticed by God.

Never forget, you are literally positioning your heart before God when you participate in an offering to Him. Remember,

> *For where your treasure is, there will your heart be also.*
>
> *Luke 12:34*

Child of God, are you beginning to capture the spirit of this matter? God does care about your finances! God immediately knows the measure from which you give, when you give, and the attitudes you have as you are giving.

That is not just my opinion; that is what the Word of God says!

So, plant this firmly in your spirit: Giving is important to God, and **He does care** how you give, but, he does seem to state a partiality to cheerful givers!

> *For God loveth a cheerful giver.*
>
> *2 Corinthians 9:7b*

Lesson 30: Money is a spiritual subject

Well over twenty percent of Holy Scripture concerns money, wealth, finances, property, lands, possessions, tithes and giving. If money is not a spiritual subject, then why is so much said about it in the Bible?

Scripture clearly shows that God wants you to have money, and to be happy with your wealth:

> *The blessing of the Lord, it maketh rich, and he addeth no sorrow with it.*
>
> *Proverbs 10:22*

> *Yea, let them say continually, Let the Lord be magnified, which hath pleasure in the prosperity of his servant.*
>
> *Psalms 35:27b*

Scripture gives clear instructions on how to increase your funds:

> *Give, and it shall be given unto you;*
>
> *Luke 6:38a*

Scripture clearly shows that when you give your money, you are performing an **ACT OF SACRED WORSHIP** to your God!

> *Bring ye all the tithes into the storehouse, that there*
> *may be (food) in mine house, and (test) me now here-*
> *with, saith the Lord of hosts, if I will not open (for)*
> *YOU the windows of heaven, and pour you out a*
> *blessing, that there shall not be room enough to*
> *receive it.*
>
> *Malachi 3:10*

Deuteronomy 26:1-12, plainly states that tithing and offerings were specific worship services before God.

You see, Satan has lied to the Body of Christ, and convinced us money is somehow evil, and definitely unspiritual. That is a lie!

Money **is** a spiritual matter.

Money is one of the acceptable scriptural offerings for worshiping your Lord.

Money is an effective tool to help bring the message of salvation to lost souls throughout the world.

Satan has lied to you about money, but when you put your money into use according to the biblical principles, and with a truly scriptural heart, money becomes a very sacred thing.

Money is literally your life. Each week when you are paid, and the money you get is the company's way of repaying you for the part of your life you spent in service to that company.

Friend, if you are sanctified holy through the blood of Christ, and you give a part of your holy life each week to your employer, then the money he gives you in exchange for your life is **holy money** and represents a portion of your total life.

Lesson 31: Give, expecting to receive

This is probably one of the most shocking and hard-to-believe Biblical principles for the Body of Christ to accept. When most Christians give, they sincerely feel they should not expect anything back for what they have given. Inside, they are saying something like this: "Lord, I don't want anything in return. I don't expect anything back. I'm just giving because I love you."

Beloved, when you give and expect nothing back, that is well and good and noble, and God will honor your heart – **but** that is **not** giving in the biblical way!

Here is the godly way to give: Give, **expecting to receive!** Notice I said this is "the godly way." When God gave, He gave with definite expectations. For instance, when God created mankind, and gave him life, He EXPECTED TO RECEIVE worship, reverence, love, service, obedience, companionship, and ultimately, sonship, back from man.

Again, when God gave His Son, Jesus, to die for us, He gave Him, expecting to receive sons and daughters in return.

The Word of God is very clear on the fact that giving is irreversibly tied to receiving:

Give, and it shall be given unto you;

Luke 6:38a

Moreover, giving is irreversibly tied to receiving back **what you give**.

Be not deceived; God is not mocked: for whatsoever a man soweth, that shall he also reap.

Galatians 6:7

Once again, let me say that's not **my** promise or **my** idea, that's God's Word!

God promises when you give your tithe and offerings, He will "Open . . . the windows of heaven, and pour you out a blessing," (Malachi 3:10b). If you have trouble with that concept, take it up with God. It is not John Avanzini's idea, it is God's Word!

Again and again, God says to give, expecting to receive so you can give even more the next time. **IT IS A GODLY WAY TO GIVE, EXPECTING TO RECEIVE.** Giving and expecting to receive, does not make you selfish. Every informed Christian would gladly give their tithes and offerings just because they love God, and want to obey His commandments, but God's ways are always better than man's ways. If He did not give back to you more abundantly than you gave, where would the money come from to take the gospel to the world?

You see, God knows what He is doing.

Stop saying that you do not expect something back from God when you give. That simply is not a biblical statement. Give, expecting to receive, so you can turn right around and be good stewards by giving even more to God's Kingdom work the next time.

There is no limit that I have found in God's Word to the abundance that you can have for the Gospel, and for your family. If you systematically persist in doing God's will in your finances.

10 TRUTHS ABOUT MONEY
IN SUMMARY

I hope by now you have realized you are reading this book because God wants you to experience a major breakthrough in the area of your finances. If you have begun to practice these concepts, God is literally beginning to strategically position you in His endtime harvest plan.

I sincerely pray that you will continue to **experience** this book line upon line, precept upon precept.

Look upon each new lesson and concept as a precious treasure, and allow the truths on each to become part of your mind. Continue to read each lesson in the morning, and then again in the evening. Feel free to go back as often as you please and reread any lesson that you have already read.

Child of God, that is God's way for you to experience change, transformation, and breakthrough!

Make no mistake about it, SATAN WANTS YOU TO BE POOR. The devil can be much more effective in neutralizing your testimony if you are financially weak and impotent. But, as the final endtime events begin to unfold around you, God wants to arm you with all His spiritual armor, and with the finances you need to effectively bring the message of salvation to a dying world.

In spiritual warfare, money is one of the necessary tools to provide desperately-needed Bibles for the entire world. Evangelistic television programs in many languages demand extensive funding. Even personal evangelism on every continent will be very expensive and will take thousands of times the money currently being allocated to world evangelism. Money is not only a spiritual subject, it is **one of the primary keys** to bringing the gospel to a lost world.

That's why Satan has tried to make up so many lies about money, and deceived so many of the saints. The "10 Truths" about money you have just studied are intended to shock your mind out of it's old ruts, and of the deceptive patterns Satan has used to feed you his mistaken ideas about money. Before you move on to the next section of this book, flip through **Section Four** and read the lesson headings – only this time say them aloud.

Really allow them to set into your spirit.

Then go back and say them again.

Child of God, remember, nothing you can ever do will more dramatically change your financial circumstances than your active

PARTICIPATION IN THE PROCESS of transforming your mind in the area of finances.

Everything else is easy.

Once you understand that God intends for you to be prosperous, and once you learn how to apply His principles of biblical economics in your life, you are on your way to a financial transformation.

This is not my "pie in the sky" promise to keep you reading – this is God's Word for you:

"Give, and it shall be given unto you."

What a glorious day this is! Scripture teaches us that Satan has been defeated for centuries, but in the area of finances, many of the saints still function as victims instead of victors.

We enthusiastically accept salvation.

We willingly receive the Holy Ghost.

Today, I believe God is birthing in you a new understanding about the gospel, an understanding that involves ACCEPTING GOD'S PROSPERITY for your life. Not just for material purposes (food, clothing, and housing), but so that you will have "more than enough" financing to meet your needs and to bring the message of Jesus Christ to a searching world.

SECTION FIVE:
5 MAJOR MISTAKES ABOUT MONEY

Lesson 32: MISTAKE # 1: The fear of money

The world you live in runs on it's own Golden Rule: whoever owns the gold makes the rules.

Did you know the Bible teaches almost the same principle? If you doubt it, read Ecclesiastes 10:19:

> *A feast is made for laughter, and wine maketh merry: but **money answereth all things***.

If you don't think that is true, just ask a mother that has to buy clothes for three or four children to go to school. Money will answer her problem.

Just ask someone who is hungry. Recently, someone said to me: "You know, Brother John, money is not very important to me."

"Brother, I know something about you," I replied. "I know you've never been hungry."

For too long the saints of God have accepted Satan's lies, and have acted as though they should "fear" having money. If you are one of those saints, then take these three key scriptures and put them up in a prominent place where you can see them **and say** them every day:

Key Scripture #1:

> *But thou shalt remember the Lord thy God: for it is he that giveth thee power to get wealth, that he may establish his covenant.*
>
> *Deuteronomy 8:18a*

Key Scripture # 2:

> *Beloved, I wish above all things that thou mayest prosper and be in health, even as thy soul prospereth.*
>
> *3 John 2*

Key Scripture # 3:

> *The blessing of the Lord, it maketh rich, and he addeth no sorrow with it.*
>
> *Proverbs 10:22*

Child of God, you do not need to fear becoming prosperous; finances are not to be feared by those who are faithful. Prosperity is God's desire for you, and as long as you function in God's commandments, you will experience His blessings in your life.

Lesson 33: MISTAKE # 2: Poverty is godly

If God's Word commanded us to be poor, we would obey.

But God's Word does not advocate poverty!

Most Christians are operating in a poverty mentality, while the devil's crowd lives the best life possible.

In Ephesians, Paul talks about "the riches of the glory of his inheritance in the saints," (Ephesians 1:18b). The Greek word for "riches" is **ploutos**. It's from a base word meaning "wealth." It literally means "money, possessions, abundance, valuable riches."

Our inheritance as sons and daughters of the King of Kings is **not** to live in poverty.

Read carefully what the scripture says. Our inheritance is to have the glory of the riches. Yet, most of us are are settling for the shells while the devil's crowd eats the peanuts.

Child of God, the earth is **the Lord's**!

God owns the cattle on a thousand hills, but he has never eaten a hamburger! What is He doing with all those cows?

They are for us!

Poverty is not godly, and it certainly is not Biblical. God wants you to open your eyes to see the invisible world, and to see the blessings He has in store for you:

> *According as his divine power hath given unto us **all***
> ***things that pertain unto life** and godliness, through*
> *the knowledge of him that hath called us to glory and*
> *virtue:*
>
> *2 Peter 1:3*

Does gasoline pertain to life? Do shoes pertain to life? Does food pertain to life? Yes!

You can lay hands on the sick, bind demons, and manifest strong spiritual power, but your Father also knows that you have need of many material things.

It is no surprise to God that your car needs tires.

It is no surprise to God that you need a coat when the temperature is below freezing.

God intends for you to have all your needs supplied according to **His riches** in glory.

In Christian circles, poverty may be popular, but it is not a Bible-founded principle: poverty goes against everything the Bible teaches, and finds its roots, causes, and effects in its author, Satan.

Lesson 34: MISTAKE # 3: The best things are free

Many times the devil invents a very spiritual sounding phrase to try and keep the church of God weak and floundering. Perhaps one of his most effective lies is "the best things in life are free."

That simply is not true: the best things in life **are not** free.

Your salvation was not free. God paid the ultimate price for it, the death of His Son, Jesus Christ!

Even Bibles come with a price: they cost money to print. Over the last 2,000 years, literally billions of dollars have been spent so men and women could have the Scriptures in their hands.

The **preaching** of the Word costs money.

Today, **television** and satellite are major vehicles to send the Word of God to other lands. Do you know how much it costs to rent just one channel on a satellite for one month? As much as $200,000. The message of the gospel is the "best thing" the world could possibly have, but it didn't come free to you or anyone else!

Someone had to pay to get it to you.

The marvelous testimony you see on your favorite television ministry program, or the wonderful sermon at your local church on Sunday did not come free! The men and women who recorded the message needed money to pay their staff, buy cameras, film, and then, air time, so you could see the message and be blessed. Your pastor is usually paid, and your church needs light, pews, paint, microphones, and many other types of equipment; somebody must pay for these needs.

You see, the best things in life are **not** free. It takes money to print and buy Bibles. It takes money to bring the gospel to other lands – whether the vehicle is a missionary, a television camera, a crusade, or a satellite – they all take money!

Mexico needs the gospel. India needs the gospel. China needs the gospel. Every home in North America needs the gospel.

And it will take money to get it to them.

Lots of it.

Child of God, the best thing in life – the gospel of Jesus Christ – did not come free!

This is not my idea, and I am not the only one who has discussed it. Many others know the need for money. The apostle paul even discussed the need for Christians to come together with the necessary funds to send missionaries to other lands.

> *How, then, shall they call on him in whom they have not believed? And how shall they believe in him of*

*whom they have not heard? And how shall they hear
without a preacher?
And how shall they preach, except they be sent?*

Romans 10: 14-15a

Lesson 35: MISTAKE # 4: Poverty will bring happiness

Money alone will never make you happy. But, neither will poverty.

Rich people commit suicide, take drugs, get drunk, and get divorced. But so do poor people. There is nothing sacred, holy, or happy about being poor. Happiness has absolutely nothing to do with the presence or absence of material things, but unhappiness can come from a lack of certain material necessities, such as food, clothing, and housing.

Happiness has to do primarily with the inner man inside of you. There's a little person who lives down inside you, and if that person is not happy, neither wealth nor poverty will bring happiness.

Your inner man can only be touched by two forces: Satan or Christ. If Satan controls your inner person, then you will be unhappy. And, if Jesus Christ has possession of your inner man, you will be happy – marvelous and miraculous things will happen to you.

You see, child of God, money, **or the lack of it**, will not change your inner man. Being poor will never make you holy or happy.

But, if you are prosperous and have a Christ-controlled inner man, He will influence the way you spend your wealth. You will meet your own basic needs and wants, and you will support world mission projects, strategic television outreaches, special needs in your local church, and other Gospel outreaches. Your money will bring you happiness because it will be accomplishing God's purpose for giving it to you.

Poverty or wealth will not bring happiness – that comes only from Jesus Christ. But, once you have Jesus Christ as the Lord of your life, you will be able to bring much happiness to the Body of Christ with money that you supply for the spread of the Gospel.

So decide now to start to prosper and be in good health. As you give to God, He will return your money back to you so you can again give to His Purposes.

69

Lesson 36: MISTAKE # 5: God does not care about finances

God **does care** about finances, but not the way the world does. Remember what we are learning about God: His ways are not the world's ways.

The worldly way of looking at a donation or gift is totally different from God's way. In the world, people who give the most money to a charitable project are honored with banquets, special plaques, ceremonial pins, and by naming buildings and hospital wings after them. They receive many outward recognitions that set them apart and reward them in accordance with how much they have given.

God takes special notice of finances and money which are donated, but in a totally different way. We have already talked about the poor widow who gave her two mites. Many others tossed much larger amounts into the treasury, but God honored the widow because she gave a **greater percentage, or a greater portion** of her total finances to God.

Jesus took very special notice of that widow. He even called the disciples to see, and then openly and publicly said to them:

Verily I say unto you, that this poor widow hath cast more in than all they which have cast into the treasury: For all they did cast in of their abundance; but she of her want did cast in all that she had, even all her living.

Mark 12: 43b, 44

Notice the difference: The world recognizes HOW MUCH you give. God recognizes **HOW MUCH you have left after you give**.

Isn't that comforting? You can depend upon God, because He does care about your finances. The world only cares about how much you gave, but God sees **how much you gave**, and **how much you have left**, and He knows how much money you need to meet your needs each day.

As you give to Him and His work, He will take care of you. He will give back to you more than enough to meet your own needs, and still have plenty left over so you can give to His work again.

God cares so much about your finances that if you will become obedient to His instructions in giving and receiving, and release His hand in your finances, He will start to work IMMEDIATELY to change your financial situation, and get you out of debt and into abundance. You see, the best way to get out of debt and financial troubles is by giving to God.

If you obey God, and give to Him, no matter how tight your finances are, or how unscriptural your giving may have been in the past, if you obey God **now** and give as He tells you to give, your financial problems will become financial blessings! God always gives back to you what you give to Him, and more.

> *Give, and it shall be given unto you; good measure, pressed down, and shaken together, and running over, shall men give into your bosom. For with the same measure that ye (measure) it shall be measured to you again.*

Luke 6:38

Remember, when you give generously to God, He is blessed by what you gave, and He is concerned about what you have left. As you give, God will provide you with more than enough to meet all of your needs and wants.

FIVE MAJOR MISTAKES ABOUT MONEY
IN SUMMARY

Do you know you live in a controlled shortage?

The diamond mine owners in South Africa meticulously control the number of diamonds which are available each year. They know that diamonds would not be very valuable if **all** the diamonds in the world appeared in the marketplace at the same time. These owners even buy back large quantities of diamonds, just to keep the number of diamonds in circulation low enough to keep the price up.

The entire point of the current oil cartel is to regulate and control the flow of oil into each country, so that a "glut" (excess supply) never drives down the price or profit on oil. The world's oil supply is in a constant state of controlled shortage to assure its high price.

Even our food production is in a controlled shortage – just ask any farmer. Even in North America, farmers are told which crops and in what quantity to grow them, as well as what to do with the surplus (the amount the government does not want to circulate to keep prices at a "fair market" price). As a result, millions of bushels of grain are stored, and many times spoil, while some Americans do not have enough to eat.

You see, to the world, money and keeping good, high prices are the main goals.

In your own spiritual walk with your personal finances, you are also living in a controlled shortage. Right now, the mints are making money so fast that the presses have to be oiled continuously to keep them from catching on fire. That is how fast they are producing money. But most of us are limited to the little bit of money in our pocket and in our checking accounts — that meager amount someone else decides is enough for us. As long as we keep our "controlled shortage" mentality, we will not see beyond what is in our pocket or bank account.

But God says He owns the silver and gold! However, in the natural world today, the control of those items is in the hands of the wicked. Without firing a shot, the saints of God are losing the financial war.

But you can unleash God's power and abundance into your financial affairs, and destroy the "controlled shortage" in your life.

> *Now unto him that is able to do exceeding abundantly*
> *above all that we ask **or think**, according to the power*
> *that worketh in us,*
>
> Ephesians 3:20

Now, all of us know how to ask for some pretty nice things. God tells us to ask, and He says He can even supply beyond what we can think. There is a "controlled shortage" in the pockets of God's children, but **we** are causing the shortage by our own limited "shortage" thinking! When will we open the eyes of our understanding?

God's storage houses are chuck full to the brim, and overflowing with His abundance. And God says, "Just ask."

Child of God, are you starting to see with spiritual eyes? We talk about "reaching the world" through great technological outreaches. Well, we can't see beyond the limitations of our own pocketbooks. If we are going to properly finance the outreach of the Kingdom of God, then we had better start seeing beyond our own limited supply, and lift our eyes and look on God's great storage houses. Psalm 84:11 says:

> *For the Lord God is a sun and shield. the Lord will*
> *give grace and glory: **no good thing will he with-***
> ***hold from them that walk uprightly.***

Is money a good thing?

YES, when it is in the control of an informed child of God!

God wants to bless you with the grace of His salvation. God wants to bless you with good health. God wants to bless you with the power, the comfort, and the gifts of the Holy Ghost.

And, He wants to bless you with abundant finances!

God is not playing games. Now is the time to bring in the endtime harvest, but we cannot reap that huge harvest without equally huge amounts of money to buy the things necessary to reap that harvest: television cameras, satellite receivers, salaries for the workers, church buildings, missionary outreaches – all that money will come from only one place, and that is from the saints of God who have taken hold of the blessings God intends for their finances.

Playboy magazine will not finance the endtime harvest.

IBM is not going to pay for it.

But, nevertheless, it will take huge amounts of money – held in the control of God's children – to reap the great endtime harvest I believe is coming very soon.

It is time for you to end the **"controlled shortage mentality."**

SECTION SIX:
THE GOOD LIFE

Lesson 37: Should Christians have luxuries?

If Lesson 1 of this book had started with this highly controversial question, I suspect you probably would have answered with a resounding "NO!" After all, don't most Christians believe that luxuries are excessive, worldly, and certainly not of God?

But now, I hope that when you read the question, you started your "new mentality" wheels turning, and answered "I'm really not sure," or better yet, "Yes! God wants me to have luxuries."

Let us look at one key example in God's Word to begin to determine an answer to this highly controversial question.

First, let's decide clearly what a luxury is. My dictionary defines a luxury as "the comforts and beautiful things of life **beyond what are really necessary**." The next definition reads, in part, "costly foods, **wines**, clothing, houses, or furniture. The things a person enjoys, usually very costly and very choice."

Child of God, for decades Christians have felt that we should have just enough to eat, an inexpensive car to ride in, and the very simplest of clothes. It was considered "holy" to just barely make it – somehow poverty was thought to be a sign of spirituality or great love for God.

But, Jesus didn't seem to function in that frame of mind. In fact, **the first miracle** He ever performed was a miracle of luxury! This miracle of luxury was of a material nature. It was at the marriage feast of Cana, as told in the second chapter of John.

When the host of this marriage feast ran out of wine, what did Jesus do? He didn't say, "Well, they've had enough. It's time for everyone to go home."

No! He made them wine, and the Apostle John reports that it was the **best wine**. Now notice, "wine" is called a luxury by my dictionary.

I think it is very important to note that the first miracle Jesus ever performed was a miracle of luxury, and He did it after everyone already had plenty of wine to drink.

God does not mind if you have nice things. The Lord Himself turned water into the finest wine.

74

Also, of the possessions Jesus personally owned, the one that the Bible describes was His cloak, the finest of coats, so lovely that the soldiers who crucified Him cast lots for it to see who would be fortunate enough to have it.

That is not all!

As you continue this study, you will discover many other similar examples of God's luxurious giving. If God Himself set the pattern, then who are we to change it?

Lesson 38: Is Jesus against you having luxuries?

One day, shortly before His crucifixion, Jesus was having dinner at a Pharisee's house, when a woman brought "an alabaster box of very precious ointment" and anointed Him. His disciples saw the action, and said:

> To what purpose is this waste? For this ointment might have been sold for much, and given to the poor.
>
> Matthew 26:8b,9

Instead of agreeing with the apostles, Jesus replied:

> Why trouble ye the woman? for she hath wrought a good work upon me.
>
> Matthew 26:10b

Once again, we see Jesus does not mind nice things. And, as He advises His apostles, He doesn't even answer their comments about waste. He instead commends the woman's actions and calls them a "good work."

Jesus appreciated the woman's kindness. In fact, He even prophesied that:

> Wherever this gospel shall be preached in the whole world, there shall (be) also this, that this woman hath done, be told for **a memorial of her**.
>
> Matthew 26:13

Child of God, there are no doubt many saints who would like to somehow take these words out of the scripture, because they do not line up with **man's** teaching of supposed humbleness through proverty and insufficiency! Jesus recognized there was enough wealth in the world for everyone, and that it was just fine for the luxurious alabaster ointment to be poured over Him. Jesus appreciated this woman's heart so much that He ordained her actions would be remembered right along with the Gospel, as a magnificent "memorial" to her!

Notice, no where did Jesus **ever** memorialize the actions of those who exemplified poverty, lack, and insufficiency. But here he memorializes this good deed done to Him with the costly ointment.

Is Jesus against luxuries? The Word of God certainly gives us no indication that He opposed them. His own actions seem to indicate He was not against them, so why are so many Christians today against luxuries?

Because they are believing **the mistaken ideas of some preacher** instead of patterning their lives and attitudes after **THE** pattern, Jesus Christ. Luxuries are not out of the question for the children of God, but remember, the greatest luxury of all is the precious blood of Jesus which was poured out without limit for all the world.

Please remember also that we should never leave the precious Gospel unpreached so that we can have our luxuries. By now you should be convinced that if you give generously into the preaching of the gospel, God will not withhold any good thing from you.

Lesson 39: You can have the good things in life

My life started to dramatically change when I **started to believe** God's promises. You see, it doesn't really matter how expensive clothing gets, or how high the price of groceries soars, because God says He will take care of you if you are taking care of those ministries that are preaching the Gospel around the world.

It is very simple. If you believe and trust God, then you will give to His work just like the Scripture says. And, as you do give to Him, here is the good news of what God promises in return:

> *But my God shall supply all your need **according to his riches** in glory by Christ Jesus.*
>
> *Philippians 4: 19*

Notice, God does not say He will supply these good things out of His riches in glory, but rather that He will supply them in accordance with His riches in glory. That means God plans to supply you according to His riches and glory, according to the good things that He enjoys.

Of course, we know that heaven is not a **"simple place "**; it is not a **poverty–ridden** place. Heaven's throne is not made out of wood and plaster and thread-bare upholstery.

The apostle John surely isn't describing a slum or a secondhand store when he gives us the description of God's riches and glory:

*And the building of the wall of it was of jasper: and
the city was pure gold, like unto clear glass. And the
foundations of the wall of the city were garnished
with all manner of precious stones. The first foundation was jasper; the second, sapphire; the third, chal-
cedony; the fourth, an emerald; The fifth, sardonyx;
the sixth, sardius; the seventh, chrysolite; the eight,
beryl; the ninth, a topaz; the tenth, chrysoprasus; the
eleventh, a jacinth; the twelfth, an amethyst. And the
twelve gates were twelve pearls; every several gate
was of one pearl: and the street of the city was pure
gold, as it were transparent glass.*

Revelations 21:18-21

God has good things, and He said He will supply your needs in
that same fashion, "according to His riches and glory." God wants
you to have good things.

Think with me. If you are doing well and prospering, and your
son or daughter was to become a partner with you, and they pleased
you very much by being great workers in the family business, would
you live in a mansion in the best part of town and let them live in a
cheap rental in the slums and barely get by?

Certainly not.

Scripture tells us that if we – as humans – know how to give
good gifts to our children, how much more will God give His
children good things.

*If ye then, being evil, know how to give good gifts unto
your children: how much more shall your heavenly
Father give.*

Luke 11:13a

Lesson 40: God wants you always abounding!

God does not talk about **barely enough** in even one place in
scripture.

*Thou preparest a table (banquet) before me in the
presence of mine enemies: thou anointest my head
with oil; **my cup runneth over**. Surely goodness and
mercy shall follow me all the days of my life: and I
will dwell in the house of the Lord forever.*

Psalm 23: 5,6

Are you starting to grasp the Spirit of God? He wants you to sit at a banquet table. He wants you anointed with costly oil. He wants your cup to overflow with good things. He wants goodness and mercy in your life!

There's no talk about running out, or running short, or doing without, or not having enough food to eat.

God is talking about abundance. He's talking about always abounding in the magnificent things He has created for us!

How many times have you stood in a store and weighed the difference between a bad suit or a good suit, a cheap dress or a well-made one? How many times have you bought a poor pair of jeans, instead of a pair that would last? How many times have you thought, "As Christians, we just can't have the best"?

Child of God, I've got a shocking statement for you: God wants you to have the best! Look at the type of clothes Jesus wore: When He was crucified, the soldiers tore up the garments of the other two men, but when it came to Jesus, they did not tear up his cloak.

> *Now the coat was without seam, woven from the top throughout. They said therefore among themselves, Let us not (tear) it, but cast lots for it, whose it shall be:*

> John 19:23b,24b

The coat Jesus wore was very fine indeed, so good that the soldiers did not want to destroy it.

Jesus wore good things, and He wants you to pattern yourself after Him.

The Apostle Paul also had a fine cloak, fine enough to specifically ask Timothy to bring it all the way from Troas to the city of Rome. It must have been very valuable to inconvenience Timothy to keep it with him all that way.

> *The cloak that I left at Troas with Carpus, when thou comest, bring with thee, .*

> 2 Timothy 4:13b

Lesson 41: A half-truth will not set you free

Only the whole truth will set you free.

Most Christians know half the truth. They know that Jesus commanded us to give up all we have and follow the Lord. And that's good teaching. I teach that. I preach that. But, there's a

78

second part to that truth – and only when you understand the second part will you really be set free.

You see, Jesus **did** say to give up all and follow Him, but He also said that if we do, He would give back one-hundred fold (literally, 100 times more than you gave), here and now.

In this lifetime.

Now, a lot of people who hear will say:

"Brother John, I just don't believe that."

Well, whether you believe it or not doesn't change the fact that the Bible teaches it!

> *Verily I say unto you, There is no man that hath left house, or brethren, or sisters, or father, or mother, or wife, or children, or lands, for my sake, and the gospel's, But* **he shall receive an hundredfold now in this time**, *houses, and brethren, and sisters, and mothers, and children, and lands, with persecutions; and in the world to come eternal life.*
>
> *Mark 10:29b,30*

There it is in black and white! You shall receive an hundredfold. Return NOW! **In this time.** Houses. Lands. Brothers. Sisters. Surely we all see that? Child of God, Jesus wants you to give all you have for Him, but only so He can give it back to you one-hundred-fold! THAT IS THE **ENTIRE** TRUTH!

God does not want you poor or homeless or without family. He only wants you to give up those things – to Him, so He can multiply them back to you.

Now, this doesn't always call for deeding all your property to the ministry. But, it does mean giving God control of all your possessions. Very seldom have I ever heard of Him asking anyone to sell everything and give to His work, but sometimes He does. One time He asked my wife and I to give up our house, and we did. He then immediately put us into a new house we liked even better, and we began to experience more abundance than we ever thought possible. But, be very careful in these decisions, as they can bring ruin into your life if they are done without God's specific instructions.

Lesson 42: Release it all; you'll get it all back

When you release everything to the Lord, He promises to return it all back to you 100 fold. That is the promise of the tenth chapter of Mark, verses 29 and 30.

God **made the promise**, now He is waiting for His people to grasp His mentality in relation to abundance, and to stop being cheated out of what is potentially theirs. You see, when you release control of your possessions unto the Lord, you do not give up a thing.

In fact, when you release it to Him, He gives it right back to you one-hundredfold! The Bible teaches it.

Read Mark 10, verses 29 and 30 again. It deals with the things we understand: houses, lands and families. Don't turn a deaf ear to what God wants you to hear in this passage. Do not let Satan lie to you even one more day that it is "holy" to be poor.

In the deepest sense, poor means to be "powerless."

If Satan can keep the saints trembling in shoes full of holes, living in rented houses, and barely able to make payments and buy groceries, then he can effectively stop the spread of the Gospel to the world. Every satellite network, every Christian television station, every-soul winning ministry, every evangelist, every Christian writer, every teacher, every Christian radio show needs money to deliver an effective gospel outreach, so you can see why Satan wants to keep the saints poor.

God says, "Release it all for my sake, and I'll give it all back to you – multiplied one hundred times!"

He is not talking about a poverty gospel. Nor is He talking about only religious things. He is talking about houses and lands! If you decide to release everything you own to God, then God will give it back to you, one-hundredfold. Notice, He wants to do it NOW! In this life. Not after you die and are in heaven.

That is God's promise – not man's. Man would never make such a promise. Only God has the resources to back it up.

God wants you to release everything – not so you will not be poor, but so He can make you 100 times richer than you were before!

That is God's way of preparing you for your dynamic part in the financing of His great endtime harvest!

Lesson 43: How to get the good life going (Part one)

Most people think the "good life" involves the material things around you – the fancy house, the nice big car, the big boat, and the seven-course dinners. Those things are nice, but they are not the "good life."

You see, the good life comes from within:

> Beloved, I wish above all things that thou mayest prosper and be in health, even as thy soul prospereth.
>
> 3 John 2

Both the conditions for prosperity, and the conditions for health, are in the well-being and the prosperity of the inner man. The good things in life do not come from the outside in; they come from within and go to the outside man.

When I write about the "good life," many unattentive Christians misunderstand what I am talking about. They think I am talking about a carnal type of lifestyle, but child of God, if you will get "the good life" inside of you, you can't help but get your life right on the outside.

The good life does not begin with the neighborhood you live in. The good life does not depend on the price of your home. The good life depends on what is going on inside of you. Remember, from the inside of you the good things that are happening begin to manifest the luxuries of life. They grow forth from the inside.

Paul was able to turn a dungeon into a palace:

> I have learned, in whatsoever state I am, therewith to be content.
>
> Philippians 4:11b

History tells us of many kings who were able to turn palaces into dungeons – because they were not right inside.

> For I rejoiced greatly, when the brethren came and testified of the truth that is in thee, even as thou walkest in the truth.
>
> 3 John 3

John did not get excited when he heard someone got a new home or fancy clothes. He rejoiced when "the truth" was in those around him. For he knew as their souls prospered, they would materially prosper and be in health.

When you operate in the truth, then you will also operate in prosperity.

Once these truths of prosperity are in your spirit, then you need to start walking in them. And when that happens, you will prosper in your health, your spirit, your soul, as well as in your financial matters.

Lesson 44: How to get the good life going (Part two)

When I talk about "the good life," please remember I am not talking about cars, houses, vacations, fancy food, and entertainment.

Cars will wear out. A house can soon become part of a slum district. The taste of fancy food lasts only a few minutes. Vacations are quickly forgotten. All of these things are nice to have in your life, but they are **not** "the good life."

If you really have the good life, your quality of life will transcend the natural and focus on the spiritual. The scripture tells us:

> *Take no thought for your life, what ye shall eat; neither for the body, what ye shall put on. The life is more than meat, and the body is more than raiment.*
>
> *Luke 12:22a-23*

God wants you to eat, and He wants you to have fine clothes, **but**, do not be anxious for them! Do not hunger after them; do not make them the Lord of your life! In these verses, God is not talking about depriving yourself of food and other nice things, He simply is asking that you keep your priorities straight.

> *But rather seek ye the kingdom of God; and **all these things** shall be added unto you.*
>
> *Luke 12:31*

Child of God, are you seeing this? Your life is more than food, drink, a nice house, and vacations. Your good life **starts** when you seek first God's kingdom and God's way, and literally put God's kingdom first. And, when you live totally in Christ, and understand that you are God's temple, and the dwelling place of the Most High, **then** you will have the nice clothes and the good car and the beautiful home. Yes, all of these things will be added unto you.

You see, it is a matter of priority.

When you walk with the things that pertain to Jesus in first place, your life is going to count; you cannot help but experience the good life, and ALL of your needs will be met.

The Gospel has never been and never will be a gospel of deprivation! God does not want to deprive you of the things you need to live, and to live abundantly. All God wants you to do is make sure you seek Him first, and then, all the other things will be added unto you.

When good times and the good life come to you, do not stop seeking Him, for as surely as you do, those things that you need that were so richly added to you will surely begin to fall away.

Lesson 45: You are half-way there!

If you have made it this far, smile! You will complete the rest of this life-transforming process. You see, in the first 45 lessons you have read and considered dynamic Biblical economic truths that may have totally shocked and upset you, as well as challenged you to rethink what the Gospel says about the riches of this planet. If you have read them with an open mind, then I believe you are being changed, and you are seeing that poverty is not a holy condition instituted by God for His special people. Rather, it is just the opposite!

You and I serve a God of abundance!

The Word of God declares Him to be so. Our God first cares about your inner man. He wants you to walk in His image and in His commandments and precepts.

Once you master that concept, "all these things" will be added unto you, but it will not be because you need a nice car, or because you desperately hunger after the best house on the block, but because God knows your heart, knows He can trust your steward-ship, and wants to give you good things.

Jesus created "the best" wine for his contemporary friends.

Jesus allowed the anointing with expensive alabaster oil.

Jesus wore a cloak so fine that the soldiers did not dare to tear it up.

Why?

Was it because Jesus felt good wine and expensive oil and fine cloaks were His life? Of course not. These things were not a priority in His life, but as long as serving His father was His main priority, then "all these things" were added.

God owns the silver and the gold on a thousand hills, so it is no big deal for Him to give some of these things to His servants, especially when He knows their heart to be pure, and knows they are not more "anxious" and excited for these material things than they are for Him and His Kingdom.

Child of God, continue your study. Your mind transformation is critical to how you will spend the remaining years on this planet, and is critical to how quickly we reap the endtime harvest for Jesus Christ.

It is only when the saints grasp these principles of Biblical economics that there will be the ability and the funds to operate full-time Christian television, the wealth needed for Christian satellites to beam the gospel around the world, the wealth needed to send preachers to foreign lands, and the wealth needed to finance every other good work God wants done in these great endtimes.

You can be sure the wicked will not do it; it is up to you and me to grasp God's life-changing principles, and apply them in our lives!

Lesson 46: Making your life RICH for God

Make no mistake about it – you and I are living in the endtimes. We are down to the final harvest. Yet, look around you. The Church of Jesus Christ does not have enough storage bins or tools to bring in the harvest. There are more than two and one-half billion souls out there who are still waiting to hear about our Jesus, and we don't have the proper funds to send them the preachers, or to beam them the television programs so they can hear the precious Gospel.

Are millions of people going to hell because God does not provide us with the resources to reach them?

Nonsense.

They are going to hell because the saints of God have not learned to lay hold of the resources that God has already provided!

Yes, God wants you abounding.

Yes, God wants you prosperous.

Yes, God wants you to have control over great wealth.

Who else can He trust? Who else will give to bring in the Kingdom? It will not be the multi-millionaire rock singers who sing Satanic songs. It won't be the pornographers who make billions of dollars by shooting pictures of little children. It won't be the drug dealers who are daily destroying the lives of so many of our precious teenagers and young adults. Surely, it will not be the liquor manufacturers.

God wants YOU in abundance because only the saints of God will take the prosperity that God has so abundantly given them and

84

USE IT as good stewards, for His Glory, and for the salvation of millions of dying souls.

Remember, God has given you the ability to prosper, and with the proper use of that prosperity, God has the ability to reach a dying world with the good news of the Gospel.

Do you understand? We need to circle the globe with the news that the King is coming, and that by His death men and women do not have to be ashamed at His coming.

I am not talking to you about another "Oh God, Bless me" club.

No. I am talking about an "Oh God, Bless me so I can give to help bring in this endtime harvest club." That's the "club" that will make a difference in our world.

If you keep running your life according to your old concepts, your old decisions about money and prosperity, then there is no way we will ever reach the lost.

It will take BREAKTHROUGHS—in our lives, and in the homes and lives of thousands of other saints before we will fully experience God's abundance and reach the world.

THE GOOD LIFE

IN SUMMARY

Most Christians do not have an agricultural mentality. They read a book like this, go to church on Sunday, give an offering to God, then wake up Monday morning complaining:

"Hey, Brother John, I gave, and it did not work."

When I hear these folks complaining, I tell them, "Then maybe you should quit serving God."

Naturally, they become very upset. "No. No. No. No. I love God. I believe in God. Why do you say such a thing, Brother John?"

"Well, if you believe in God, do you believe in His Word?"

Again, they become rather upset. "Yes. Of course I do."

"Then wait. Whatever you have planted will come up," I reply.

You see, giving to God is like a farmer planting seed. The farmer does not wake up the next morning after planting the seed to run out to his field, and yell: "It didn't work! It didn't work! My wheat seed didn't come up."

Today, you and I function in an industrial mentality. Everything is instant. Instant printing. Instant fried chicken. Instant banking.

But, child of God, the principles of Biblical economics are literally agricultural, farming principles, not industrial principles.

When you sow, you will reap, but not tomorrow! In due season.

It takes faith and patience to bring these God-given principles to their fullest potential. Plant your seed regularly, and at first it will look futile. But, there comes a day when you have many money seeds of prosperity planted, and all of a sudden the harvest starts to grow so fast that you can barely contain it.

You must have a farm mentality to understand this, because that is the way God sends His riches back to us: We plant, and in due season, we harvest.

A few months ago I was driving through South Africa and I noticed orange colored dirt fields for miles. The dirt was turned, the rows were neat, but there were no crops. I asked my companion to explain the empty fields: "Those are wheat fields. They are waiting for rain," he told me. You see, the seed was in the ground. The field was already planted, but they were just waiting for rain. When the rain hits, it will turn those hillsides into wheat harvests!

God has given you the seeds in your hands to get prosperous. Here they are:

> But thou shalt remember the Lord thy God: for it is he that giveth thee power to get wealth, **that** he may establish his covenant which he sware unto thy fathers as it is this day.
>
> *Deuteronomy 8:18*

God has given (you already have it!) the POWER to get wealth so that His covenant could be established on earth. But you must use that power with a farmer's mentality. God is not the great spiritual slot machine in the sky. You do not put in $100 and instantly get back $1000. No, you plant $100 into God's Gospel, God's work, and let that seed grow and mature and develop so that "in due season" God will return to you many times what you planted.

When He returns the harvest, go ahead and eat some of the seed. Go ahead and buy a nice car or a new suit, or whatever you desire, but be sure you save enough seed to abundantly replant again, to put MORE MONEY SEEDS into the Gospel, so GOD CAN RETURN TO YOU even more of His abundance to plant and reap again in constantly increasing harvests for His endtime work.

SECTION SEVEN:
THE ABUNDANCE OF GOD!

Lesson 47: Creation . . . in abundance

We serve an abundant God. His creation is in abundance all around us: abundant water, land, mountains, animals, plants, trees, insects, and much more. It only makes sense that He would desire for our lives to abound "exceedingly abundantly" too.

The Word of God agrees:

> Now unto him that is able to do exceeding abundantly **above all that we ask or think**, according to **the power that worketh in us,**
>
> Unto him be glory in the church by Christ Jesus throughout all ages, world without end. Amen.
>
> *Ephesians 3:20,21*

There are three very critical points contained in this scripture:

First, God not only wants to give us more than we can ask for, He clearly states He wants to give us more than we can even think about! It is difficult enough for us to understand God giving us more than we can ask for, but even when you stretch your imagination as far as it will go, you will still come short of God's desire for us. Yet, He takes us far beyond our desires, all the way to the incomprehensible measure of MORE THAN WE CAN EVEN IMAGINE!

Second, God wants to give us this unlimited blessing "according to the power that worketh in us." Our relationship with God is critical here. God's **promises** will operate through us only to the degree we allow His **power** to operate in us. We must be totally submissive to His will in our lives to break into the wonderful realm of "above all that we (can) think!"

Third, we see the true purpose of this abundance: "Unto him be glory!" Abundance, above all we ask or think, is primarily to bring glory to God. You cannot effectively penetrate your community for God from a position of poverty or selfishness. Contrary to the beliefs of many Christians, God intends abundance for you and me – so we will not be hindered from bringing glory to Him. Remember, this realm of more than we can ask or think belongs to those who seek His Glory, not their own.

When you walk in the abundance of God, and go beyond simply having your needs met, you can do some powerful and wonderful things for the Kingdom of God. You can more easily further God's plan when you can get past basic needs such as rent, groceries, utilities, and car payments, and enter into a dimension more than you can ask or think, where there are more than enough resources available for all the ministries God lays on your heart.

God wants to give you MORE than you can ask, MORE than you can imagine, because His plan for you is infinitely greater than you can ask or imagine!

Most Christians cannot think in this realm. They have a hard time believing that God wants to use them in financing the endtime harvest because the devil has crippled their divine imagination with thoughts of **impossibility and insufficiency**.

Now, by faith you can break out of the devil's insufficiency thinking, and God will open new visions of abundance that exceed all you can ask or think.

God wants you to flourish in His abundance so you will have more than enough to finance the endtime harvest.

Lesson 48: Walking . . . in abundance

How do you start to walk in abundance?

You have already taken THE FIRST STEP:

> **You now know that you know, that you know, that God intends abundance for His children.**

Once you KNOW that God desires abundance and MORE THAN YOU CAN EVEN THINK for you, then you are ready to take the second step:

Right now, **form an effective giving and receiving covenant with God.** Raise your hands and pray this prayer aloud to the Lord:

> "Dear Lord, I sincerely desire to give an ever increasing portion of wealth to you for the financing of your great endtime harvest. Today, I solemnly pledge to become much more involved in the spreading of the gospel by starting your Biblical seeding process in my life now. I will begin by faithfully (weekly, monthly) giving $_____ into your work (state an amount – it should be over the amount of your tithe).
>
> "Lord, beginning today, by faith, I am planting these money seeds to start your flow of abundance in my life. I promise that as you multiply a money harvest back to me, I will always reinvest a generous portion back into the spreading of your Gospel.

"Thank you, Lord, for revealing these Biblical principles of economics to me. I am now determined to unleash these bold new principles into my own life. I thank you now, Lord, for your abundance which this positive action on my part will bring to pass soon. Amen."

Now take the critical third step: **Exercise the covenant.** Child of God, not only must you KNOW God's principles of biblical economics, and make a strong COVENANT with God, you MUST FAITHFULLY EXERCISE this covenant; **you must now put these principles to work**.

Begin giving today, and God will begin blessing and returning to you larger and larger amounts of wealth for you to liberally reinvest into the Gospel ministry.

> *Give, and it shall be given unto you;*   Luke 6:38a
> *There is (he) that scattereth, and yet increaseth; and there is (he) that withholdeth more than is (fitting), but it tendeth to poverty.*
> *The liberal soul shall be made fat: and he that watereth shall be watered also himself.*
>
>   Proverbs 11:24,25

Start being a great receiver by giving generously to the Lord's work right now.

Give to your local church. Give to Christian television. Give to those great ministries God puts on your heart. Always give remembering your increase does not come from the specific ministry you give to – because you are really giving to God, and He has no limit on the ways he will choose to give funds back to you.

Lesson 49: Prosperity . . . in abundance

God's thoughts are not your thoughts. In the natural realm, the proper way to achieve abundance is to keep all the wealth you can, carefully tucking it away in a safe place, and drawing a moderate rate of interest so that it can gradually grow into even more wealth.

But that is not God's plan for the greatest increase in wealth!

In God's word, we read that we must first give away that which we want to accumulate. If you desire abundance in finances, you must give away a part of your finances. Paul wrote about this principle in Philippians 4:15-17:

> *Now ye Philippians know also, that in the beginning of the gospel, when I departed from Macedonia, no church communicated with me as **concerning giving***

89

and receiving, but ye only. For even in Thessalonica ye sent once and again unto my necessity. Not because I desire a gift: but I desire fruit (finances) that may abound to your account.

To flourish in God's prosperity and bask in His abundance, you must first begin to give away, creating a new life-giving flow to your finances.

Stagnant finances cannot draw new money to you. Remember, Paul said **giving and receiving** are inter-related and interdependent upon each other. I know by now this doesn't seem contradictory to you. Surely you are beginning to realize the true meaning of this passage:

For my thoughts are not your thoughts, neither are your ways my ways, saith the Lord. For as the heavens are higher than the earth, so are my ways higher than your ways, and my thoughts than your thoughts.

Isaiah 55:8,9

Unfortunately, even with this clear disclosure of God's viewpoint, most preachers in the various Christian churches are not thinking the thoughts of God on this subject. For so long, most of our church leaders have preached that it is wrong to seek prosperity, although these same church leaders often had no problem befriending and giving special attention to the few saints who had prosperity and abundance.

But these thoughts are not God's. In Scripture, He plainly declares:

But thou shalt remember the Lord thy God: for it is he that giveth thee power to get wealth, that he may establish his covenant which he sware unto thy fathers, as it is this day.

Deuteronomy 8:18

If God did not desire for you to prosper, He would not have given you the power to get wealth. But, don't get upset if your friends and business acquaintances don't instantly begin to practice these wonderful new principles of abundance. Remember, God's thoughts are surely not man's thoughts.

The Apostle John prayed 2,000 years ago that you would receive God's best:

Beloved, I wish above all things that thou mayest prosper and be in health, even as thy soul prospereth.

3 John 2

Lesson 50: Abound in faithfulness

A faithful man shall abound with blessings:

Proverbs 28:20a

Isn't that a wonderful verse of scripture? But, what must we do to be considered a faithful person?

If you want to become faithful, you must first promise to be faithful to something. You see, not until you make a promise, and then keep it, have you proven yourself to be faithful.

Think back to Lesson 48. In that lesson, you promised God to begin planting a specific amount of money into the Gospel. Now, as you faithfully keep that promise, God will consider you to be a faithful person, and He will allow your life to begin to abound with ever-increasing blessings.

Traditionally we have been taught false concepts concerning our lives abounding with blessings. We have been led to believe that the blessings God promises are only **spiritual** blessings, or blessings which pertain to our spiritual relationship with God – surely they are not financial or material blessings!

Child of God, the context of this verse alone quickly shows us that the blessings of the faithful men **are** material and financial. Notice this verse:

He that tilleth his land shall have plenty of bread: but he that followeth after vain persons shall have poverty enough.

Proverbs 28:19

There is no question that God cares about you having spiritual blessings, but He also desires, with just as much fervor, that you "shall have plenty of bread," a symbol of all the material needs you have. He is not just talking about spiritual blessings – He is talking about basic needs and wants.

Notice that those who are not faithful, who follow after vain persons, or operate a futile plan, **shall be poor**. When God speaks here of abounding in blessings, the context of this passage indicates God is talking about much more than spiritual benefits: He is referring to bread for your table, a car for transportation, a home for shelter, **and** finances to reach a dying world.

If you are FAITHFUL in keeping your promises to God, then He will be faithful in keeping His promises to you. Remember, He said in Luke 6:38 that if you give to Him, He will give back in greater abundance to you. That is God's promise for the faithful man or woman.

91

Be faithful in your pledges to God. Give as much or more than you promised, and give it when you said you would. As you obey this principle of biblical economics, God will be faithful to His promises and abundantly bless you.

Lesson 51: Poverty is NOT godly

Many of you reading this book are living in poverty or great need right now. Most of you are in a financial wilderness, and it must almost crush your heart to read page after page about the abounding prosperity of Jesus Christ.

I do not want to hurt you with this message, and surely neither does God. He wants you to abound! So, let's look at a situation of deep poverty that was changed forever by the same truths I have been teaching you lesson after lesson in this book.

In the eighth chapter of 2 Corinthians, we read that the Church of Macedonia was in **deep, deep poverty.** They were so poor that when they put together a financial gift for the gospel ministry, they had to beg the apostle Paul, who knew of their "great trial of affliction," and "their deep poverty," to receive it, "(Beseeching) us with much entreaty that we would receive the gift," (2 Corinthians 8:4). Yet, because **that church understood the principles of biblical economics,** it prospered so much that the testimony was used to encourage other churches to give.

This pattern takes place throughout God's Word. We've already seen the widow of Zarephath in 1 Kings, chapter 17. She was in deep poverty until she cast off fear and decided to give to God's ministry. When she gave of her food, she became a prosperous woman, with more than enough to meet her own needs.

If poverty was God's will for His children, then when they were deeply into poverty, He surely would not bring his faithful servants out of their circumstances! If it were godly to be poor, God would not have blessed the church at Macedonia so greatly that they "abounded unto the riches of their liberality" (2 Corinthians 8:2).

If poverty were godly, then God would not have given the widow of Zarephath so much that she and her household "did eat many days. And the barrel of meal (was not used up,) neither did the cruse of oil fail," (1 Kings 17:15b,16a)

Child of God, if you are in need, and do not have enough to eat or to meet your daily needs, then by all means follow the principles of biblical economics the widow at Zarephath and the Church at

Macedonia followed:

> *The liberal soul shall be made fat: and he that water-*
> *eth shall be watered also himself.*
>
> *Proverbs 11:25*

Remember, God can change your poverty to prosperity, even when you are in deep poverty, or down to your last few crumbs. He did it in the Bible days, and He will do it for you today.

Lesson 52: Giving . . . in abundance

Right now, you may consider yourself to be a fairly generous giver. You probably are faithful with your tithe, and even give generous offerings when prompted by a well-presented need, or the Holy Spirit.

But, Child of God, I want you to enter a whole new dimension of giving and receiving; I want you to experience a bold new realm far beyond what now seems substantial to you.

You see, your giving horizon – the highest, greatest and most blessed experience of giving and receiving you can imagine now – is merely the starting point for a whole new giving experience that is beginning to take form in your spirit today.

Child of God, realize that the world is laid off in stratas, actual layers of awareness in our potential for accomplishment. Now we all know Satan is trying to keep us from rising above our current giving strata. He wants to keep us in a low strata of awareness, far short of what God intends for us, and far short of what you desire to attain.

But, now is the strategic time for you to make up your mind you are going to think some bold new thoughts, and literally make some new financial breakthroughs.

When I was going to Bible college, once a month, I went down to the government welfare office in Springfield, Missouri, and got my box of surplus commodity cheese and government Spam, and those awful-tasting rolled oats.

The first thing I ate was the cheese. Then the Spam. And, finally, for the last 28 days of the month, I ate awful-tasting rolled oats. Then one day, I realized most folks were eating better food than my rolled oats.

They were simply living on another economic strata, a financially-superior level, right there in the same town. I came to find out there was a cheese-and-meat crowd who were passing the cheese and meat they didn't eat right down to me!

You see, there are different stratas in life, and as long as Satan can keep you from climbing out of the stratum you are presently in, he can keep you from having the surplus you need to give to the preaching of the Gospel.

We do not have to wait for some millionaire to go out and get saved to fund God's endtime harvest. The truth of the matter is that when you fully realize the new strata of abundance God has for you, and when you realize you can rise up out of the dimension you are in (even if your current status feels like abundance now), you can reach a far more prosperous strata.

No matter what level you are currently in, it is time to move into a new dimension of abundance. Remember, God has a divine plan for your life, and you can be sure it isn't a cheap, second-class plan. Begin now to prayerfully elevate your thoughts and your finances to a new dimension, asking God to guide you into a new strata of plenty.

Remember, you are being changed from glory to glory, or literally from one financial level to another new one. God wants you to go from glory to glory in your finances, so you can consistently increase the amount you give to preach His Gospel throughout the world.

Lesson 53: How much does it cost to live in heaven?

How much do you think it will cost to live in heaven for one year? Will you have to buy food? Is rent high there? Will there be doctor bills?

Of course not! Everyone knows in heaven there will be no need for money for houses, lands, or material possessions. We will not need money to rent our heavenly mansions. We will not need money to repair our heavenly harps. Money simply will have no value or purpose in heaven.

If this is the case, then, child of God, let me ask you a much more serious question:

Why does the Bible speak of increase in your money and material wealth, and of becoming rich by the blessings of God? Why does the Bible talk about prosperity at all?

Obviously, material blessings are of no value in heaven; they will be completely worthless once you enter the Pearly Gates.

Surely God knows money, wealth, and prosperity have to do with activity going on right now on this earth. Prosperity, money, and wealth are to be used in the here and now.

Listen carefully to the words of Jesus as He promises increase of goods beyond your wildest dreams, not after you get to heaven, but right here and now:

> There is no man that hath left house, or brethren, or
> sisters, or father, or mother, or wife, or children, or
> lands, for my sake, and the gospel's,
> But he shall receive **AN HUNDREDFOLD NOW IN
> THIS TIME**, **houses**, and brethren, and sisters, and
> mothers, and children, and **lands**, . . . and in the
> world to come eternal life.
>
> Mark 10:29b,30

Child of God, houses and lands will have no value in eternity. The only place a new house will mean anything to you is "NOW, IN THIS TIME!" The only place lands will mean anything to you is "NOW, IN THIS TIME!" They have no value in heaven!

Now granted, God is deeply concerned about your spiritual blessings, but always remember, He is also vitally concerned about your material blessings NOW, in this life.

Please, keep the new thoughts you are gaining in their proper perspective with the Word. This is probably a good time to remember once again Deuteronomy 8:18:

> But thou shalt remember the Lord thy God; for it is he
> that giveth thee power to get wealth, that he may
> establish his covenant which he sware unto thy
> fathers, as it is this day.

Houses, lands, money, wealth: all of these come to the generous giver of the Gospel, so he or she can give again even more generously to reach the world with the Gospel of the Kingdom of God.

Lesson 54: God is the author of abundance

God wants you to abound, and it is **HIS BLESSINGS** that enable you to accumulate wealth. Here is a KEY PRINCIPLE in biblical economics:

> The blessing of the Lord, it maketh rich, and he
> addeth no sorrow with it.
>
> Proverbs 10:22

God is the author of your abundance; it is part of being blessed by Him. He has put down a firm foundational plan in Scripture to teach you HOW to become rich, without sorrows! (Keep in mind these are God's words, not the words of a man.)

But why has God given us this clear plan for increasing in wealth? Surely, it is not just so you can buy a nice home and drive a new car, (although God is not opposed to you having good things).

But, God's basic desire for you is that you grow beyond simply being blessed, and BECOME A BLESSING to others.

In Romans 12, verses 6 and 8, we see that giving is a spiritual gift, and the ability to give liberally to finance the endtime harvest of souls, will bless people in precisely the same way as prophecy, teaching, exhortation or even speaking in tongues.

> *Having then gifts differing according to the grace that is given to us, let us use them: if prophecy, let us prophesy in proportion to our faith;*
>
> **He who gives, (let him do it) with liberality;**
>
> Romans 12:6 & 8b NKJ

We continuously hear about the gift of prophecy. The gift of teaching. The gift of exhortation. The gift of tongues.

But, when was the last time you heard a sermon on the gift of giving? But it is there, in black and white, in the 12th chapter of Romans, and God gave it to us.

Virtually every great work of God has to have a FAITHFUL GROUP OF MINISTERS behind it that MINISTER WITH THEIR FINANCES. But, child of God, surely by now it is becoming clear that you will need "more than enough" to have a giving ministry. That is why God is the author of abundance, and HIS BLESSINGS can make you rich, without sorrow.

Let's be realistic. You cannot operate in an effective giving ministry from poverty or want or shortage or insufficiency. Remember, the only way out of the four inhibitors of prosperity— poverty, want, shortage, and insufficiency—is generous giving. Remember, too, God will always give whatever you give back to you again.

Be faithful over a little, and He will give you a lot to be faithful over. If you exercise faithfulness and patience, eventually, you will find yourself in the MINISTRY OF FINANCES, and you will become a banker for God!

THE ABUNDANCE OF GOD!

IN SUMMARY

When I was a traditional Baptist preacher, I would have never been filled with the Holy Spirit if I had stopped to think about it. You see, everything that was dear to me was on the line, including possibly my marriage! If you marry a Baptist girl and she wakes up one morning and catches you in a corner speaking in tongues, you could have serious marriage problems!

There came a moment, however, when I had to say: "Yes, the fullness of the Holy Spirit is of God, and I want that POWER;" I took it before I could reason it out with my traditional, doctrinal mentality and talk myself out of it.

In this book you are receiving great amounts of "new" information, much of which you have never heard before. But, believe me, you will not have a breakthrough, or receive all God has for you in the area of your finances, until **you** reach out and take it!

> *And from the days of John the Baptist until now the kingdom of heaven suffereth violence, and **the violent take it by force**.*   *Matthew 11:12*

The Kingdom of heaven is taken by force. The violent men of this verse do not wait around until someone cuts them a small slice of heaven, they take it by force themselves. They press upon and lay hold of it. They put their hands out before anyone else and grab for what they want. That is the new attitude the children of God must have in their finances.

You cannot enter into a new dimension of prosperity by being passive. It takes aggressiveness. You must violently snatch your mind out of the old ruts of your old thinking, and with deliberate force press into the new-found blessings of God's abundance!

I know you are grasping the truth of what I'm telling you: I am talking to you about breaking out of the old ruts, of moving into a new level, a new strata of life. Right now, your most distant horizon of abundance forms the foundation for an entire new life. God has something big for your life, but you must be willing to take it by force.

You must be willing to do battle and break out of your old concepts. You must be willing to fight the resistance you will feel from the devil and from your old insufficiency mentality. You will have to fight the "Oh,-here-we-go-again" feeling that comes over you when your preacher calls for the offering, when you hear an appeal on a telethon, or receive the monthly ministry donor letter.

You must fight to achieve a new level of understanding, and realize that every offering is an opportunity to plant the seeds that will bring forth more fruit, so in turn, you can plant even more seeds into YOUR MINISTRY OF GIVING! Remember, whenever you give in an offering to meet the budget, you are also giving to help meet **your** own needs you will have a few days or a few weeks from now.

You must fight the urge to give only $5 when God is clearly telling you in your spirit to give $50. Child of God, you will only make this breakthrough in your finances through a violent overthrow of your old thinking and the forceful implanting of the mind of Christ into your giving.

You must continue to change the way you think.

For, as you begin to live more in God's abundance, you will receive greater abundance in your life. Continue to violently react to the poverty in your life. It is time to break out of that struggle, and press through to the breakthrough. For years, I sat around passively hoping, waiting for something to happen. Nothing did. Finally, I had to decide to get violent, and by force, breakthrough.

If that is what is in your heart right now, you have made the decision to change your life. You've made up your mind that you are going to have a breakthrough, but you will have to get violent to get it.

The hard truth is that we do not have a chance of reaching this world with the Good News of Jesus, His love, His new kind of living until many more of the saints of God literally revolutionize their thinking and violently possess, by force, what God has for us.

Say this statement aloud with me: "Yes, I can have abundance so that I can sow it into the things of God, and the lives of others."

Aren't you glad you are learning that God wants you to be blessed, and rich? Continue to sieze your blessing, so you can operate the ever-increasing gift of GIVING even more strongly everyday.

SECTION EIGHT
FIRST THINGS FIRST

Lesson 55: What is God's order?

To understand and apply God's principles of biblical economics so you can have AN ACTIVE, EFFECTIVE MINISTRY OF GIVING to finance the endtime harvest, you must first establish God's proper spiritual order in your life.

God, the Father, should be first. There's no question about that.

> *Jesus said unto him, Thou shalt love the Lord thy God with all thy heart, and with all thy soul, and with all thy mind.*
> *This is the first and great commandment.*
> *Matthew 22: 37,38*

That's conclusive. God should be first. There's probably not a single soul in all of Christianity who would disagree with that. I do not know of one doctrine, one church, one preacher, one teacher or one philosopher who would argue this principle.

But, to make any MAJOR BREAKTHROUGH in the spiritual area of finances, your spiritual priorities must be absolutely straight. **God must be first in every aspect of your life,** not just in your passive agreement, but in your daily **actions**.

He must come before money: If you spend three minutes a day praying, and ten hours a day going after more money, then who is your God?

He must come before your own career: If you spend all of your waking hours concentrating on career moves, and no time asking God for His will, then who is your God?

He must come before your own pleasure: If all of your leisure time is spent pursuing pleasure, reading magazines and watching television, while the Bible gathers dust on the dining room table, then who is your God?

Yes, God must come even before your precious spouse or children. Family picnics and other family outings assume their proper priority only when God is the head of your household.

GOD IS FIRST!

> *I am the Lord thy God, which have brought thee out of the land of Egypt, out of the house of bondage.*
> *Thou shalt have no other gods before me.*
> *Exodus 20:2,3*

If you want to have an ACTIVE, EFFECTIVE MINISTRY OF GIVING, you must prayerfully and carefully make sure your priorities are clear and in scriptural order. If there is any area of your life that ranks above God, then repent of that wrong emphasis, and prayerfully put your heart in proper order.

Remember, Jesus Himself put this into focus in the book of Matthew, chapter 6, verse 33:

> *But seek ye first the kingdom of God, and his right-*
> *eousness; and all these things shall be added unto*
> *you.*

This careful ordering of our priorties is the way to bring forth the things we need.

Lesson 56: God is first. Who is second?

Many people get very upset when they find out who should come after God in your list of priorities: YOU!

That's right. The Bible declares YOU are second:

> *And the second is like unto it, Thou shalt love thy*
> *neighbour as thyself.*
> *On these two commandments hang all the law and the*
> *prophets.*
>
> *Matthew 22:39,40*

Most of us are pretty good about taking care of ourselves. Each month we manage to make the house payments, the car payments, and meet most of our needs, including entertainment, education, and even clothing.

We know fairly well how to love ourselves second, but the hard part is that we are supposed to love our neighbor in the same way!

You are dedicated to meeting your own needs, but the Word says you need to be dedicated to meeting the needs of the world as well. Your neighbor is every man, woman, boy and girl in the world, irregardless whether they are saved or lost.

The Church understands clearly who to love first: God. And, we love ourselves second: we manage to meet our own needs.

But, if Jesus placed your fellow man in a position equal to your own, then to fulfill that commandment (the second most important commandment), you and I would have to be conscious of our neighbor's specific needs, whether it be spiritual, physical, or financial.

To be in the center of God's will and not block any of the good things God has for you, you must have as much concern for the people in the world as you have for yourself. God wants YOU to prosper so you can help others around you to prosper spiritually, physically, and financially!

If you get these two priorities straight, child of God, it won't be long before you will be in the center of God's will, and will begin to optimize the flow of God's abundance in your life. If all the saints caught this vision, it would be only a very short time until we would see the precious people of the world being drawn nearer to Jesus.

111 John 2 speaks of the wish or prayer of John for our prosperity and our health, but notice that both these benefits are linked to our soul's prosperity:

> *Beloved, I wish above all things that thou mayest*
> *prosper and be in health, even as thy soul prospereth.*

There is no prosperity for the soul that neglects the two greatest commandments. Put God first, and ourselves and our neighbor second.

Remember, the soul that prospers brings material prosperity and health to its owner, and the soul that sins and rebels shall die.

> *The soul that sinneth, it shall die.*

Ezekial 18:20a

Lesson 57: What about "The Church"?

Today, I want to ask you another question concerning priorities: Which comes first: your job, your family, or your place of worship?

Opinions differ.

Most Christians would probably pick their family. But, if we can believe the Word, that is not the right answer.

When Isaac moved to Beersheba to live (Genesis 26), the first thing he did was to **build an altar for worship**.

> ***And he builded an altar there, and called upon the***
> ***name of the LORD,*** *and pitched his tent there: and*
> *there Isaac's servants digged a well.*

Genesis 26:25

The second thing He did was **to set up the place where his family would live**: he pitched his tent. Now, Isaac was a well digger, so the third thing he did was supervise the digging of a well.

Church.

Family.

Profession.

101

Isaac put his place of worship first, his family second, and the prosperity and well-being of his profession third.

In order to enjoy God's best, we must put God's priorities in place in our lives. The place where you receive your spiritual meat must have a top priority in your life. It may be your local church, a radio or television ministry, or a major literature ministry. Wherever you receive your spiritual nourishment, that place deserves a priority in your heart and in your finances.

Since you are now unleashing God's abundant blessings in your life through the POWER of giving, give top priority first to your spiritual storehouse – the place where you receive your spiritual nourishment. Make out your tithe and offering check first, before you even pay one bill. Set aside the firstfruits for your God.

Isaac put his place of worship first.

You should follow that pattern in your life too.

Lesson 58: Pay bills or tithe first?

To have AN ACTIVE, EFFECTIVE MINISTRY OF GIVING in your life, not only must your priorities concerning God be proper, but your priorities in your giving must be clear.

A major question many Christians ask as they begin to put their financial house in order is:

"Do I tithe before or after I pay my bills?"

Many people will pay all of their bills, and then, after all of the bills are distributed, they will tithe to God out of the remaining money. That may be common practice, but child of God, it is not what the Bible teaches in Deuteronomy 26, verses 2, 10, and 12a.

> *That thou shalt take of **the first of all the fruit** of the earth, which thou shalt bring of thy land that the LORD thy God giveth thee, and shalt put it in a basket, and shalt go unto the place which the LORD thy God shall choose to place his name there.*
>
> *And now, behold, I have brought **the firstfruits** of the land, which thou, O LORD, hast given me. And thou shalt set it before the LORD thy God, and worship before the Lord thy God.*
>
> *When thou hast made an end of tithing . . .*

The process of bringing the FIRSTFRUITS (before the bills) to God is called the tithe. God's Word says you should tithe first, before you do anything else with your fruits (finances)!

Now, some of you might say:

"But, Brother John, if I tithe first, I won't have enough to pay my bills."

Think about how full of unbelief that statement is. If you believe that, then you are not believing that the tithe will open the windows of heaven to you.

You see, tithing establishes a new relationship between you and God. It brings you before the open windows of heaven. Literally, this means that the treasure house of God is now open to you. If you put God first as He says to do, then surely God will bless you.

To break through into abounding finances, you must not listen to the devil on this matter. He would have you become fearful and pay your bills first. And, as sure as you do, more times than not when you have completed the bill-writing exercise, there will not be enough to tithe, much less to make an additional good offering before God.

Please be wise enough to see that if you tithe and make offerings, after all the bills are paid, you are leaving yourself at the mercy of your bills. With this action, your tithe and offerings are subject to and under the control of your bills.

But, if you tithe first, and give a generous offering, then your bills become subject and under the control of your tithes and offerings.

Remember, Malachi 3:10-11 speaks of open windows for tithing, and uninterrupted harvests for your offerings. As long as you have bills, **always** keep them in their proper place behind the tithe. Make God's business first and foremost, and He will make your business first.

Lesson 59: Do you pay the men of God before yourself?

The Bible instructs a teacher to teach the entire Word of God, no matter what the situation. In this lesson, I'm really trusting God that you will HEAR HIS WORD. Tremendous future blessings pivot on how you receive this lesson.

Let's restate the question:

"Who do you pay first, the man of God, or yourself?"

Prayerfully read what I have to say before you answer.

First, you need to think about the many men and women of God there are who spiritually bless your life. You have the pastor of your church, Bible teachers, evangelists, missionaries, television and radio ministers, and many, many more.

Read 1 Timothy 5:17 and 18:

> *Let the elders that rule well be counted worthy of double honour, especially they who labor in the word and doctrine.*
> *For the scripture saith, Thou shalt not muzzle the ox, that treadeth out the corn. And, the laborer is worthy of his reward.*

The laborer (ordinary worker) is worthy of his hire, but those who labor in the Word or in Christian ministry are worth DOUBLE pay.

Pay is the thing that this scripture is concerned about.

Elijah understood this principle when he commanded the hungry widow of Zarephath to give her last bit of corn to the man of God,

> *But make me thereof a little cake **first**, and bring it unto me, and **after** make for thee and thy son.*
>
> *1 Kings 17: 13 b*

Elijah told the widow to make the cake first for the man of God, not because he didn't care about her needs, but he knew that as she provided for the servant of God, God would provide for her and her family.

And HE did!

> *She, and he, and her house, did eat for many days.*
> *And the barrel of meal (was not used up), neither did the cruse of oil fail,*
>
> *1 Kings 17: 15b,16 a*

The Bible teaches very clearly that the men of God who minister to you in your life need to receive high priority when you begin to distribute the dollars that you put into the Gospel.

Before you conclude this lesson, before you pass judgment on this new concept, please hear one more verse:

> *Let him that is taught in the word (share) unto him that teacheth in all good things.*
>
> *Galatians 6: 6*

Lesson 60: The primary truth: giving goes before receiving

You have been learning in the last few days that God sets priorities. In this lesson, I want to emphasize the most elementary priority of all in the principles of biblical economics. I almost left it unmentioned, but God said to most surely include it:

GIVING ALWAYS GOES BEFORE RECEIVING!

The world would have you believe that first you receive, and then you give. So many times I have heard good, honest, sincere Christians say:

"Oh, Brother John, when I receive a million dollars, or some large sum, I'm going to give a great amount to the work of the Lord! You just watch. I know that I will."

Well, strangely, the Bible contradicts that bit of human reasoning. The Bible says you must be faithful in a little, or you will never have the opportunity to be faithful in a lot:

He that is faithful in that which is least is faithful also in much: and he that is unjust in the least is unjust also in much.

Luke 16:10

Now read this carefully:

Waiting for abundance before starting to give will not insure the giving of large gifts: it will actually insure just the opposite: you will not give at all.

First things come first: If you want to receive from God, you must first begin to give. The Bible clearly teaches this over and over again, throughout the entire book. Luke 6:38 says give first, then it will be given to you. Malachi 3:10 says tithe first, then God will open the windows of heaven, and pour out a blessing.

Even unsaved farmers know this primary principle: you must sow before you can reap. You will **never** hear a farmer say:

"I'm not going to do any planting just yet. God must first give me a harvest of wheat, **then** I'll plant my seed in the field."

Every farmer knows that simply will not happen. He must first plant seeds, no matter how few he has, and **then** he will get back a harvest.

Does the Lord give you salvation first, **and then** you give your heart to HIM? Of course not. First YOU GIVE your heart to Him, and then HE GIVES you eternal life.

God's principle of first planting, then reaping, is firmly

entrenched in every aspect of life, from Genesis to Revelation, from farming to the propogation of every species.

THERE IS NO HOPE OF INCREASE WITHOUT SEEDING!

Remember what Solomon said:

> *To every thing there is a season, and a time to every purpose under the heaven:*
> *A time to be born, and a time to die;* ***a time to plant, and a time to pluck up that which is planted.***
>
> Ecclesiastes 3:1,2

FIRST THINGS FIRST

IN SUMMARY

The only recorded time when someone asked Jesus how to be saved, it was a rich young ruler who asked: "Good Master, what shall I do to inherit eternal life?"

Amazing as it may seem, Jesus preached a money sermon to that young man. He told the young man to go sell all he had and give it to the poor and follow Him!

Why did Jesus do this? Do you think it was because He wanted that young fellow to be poor?

NO! A thousand times NO!!!

It was because Jesus wanted Him to have his priorities clear! If the young ruler would have agreed to give up his riches for the gospel's sake, Jesus would have surely given the riches back to him greatly increased. Scripture clearly teaches this in Mark 10:28-30, (read it at your leisure). Also, scripture teaches that you cannot possibly go broke giving to the poor. Hear the word of God:

> *He that hath pity upon the poor lendeth unto the Lord; and that which he hath given will he pay him again.*
>
> Proverbs 19:17

Now remember, God must be your first priority. When His priority is established over your money, then God can begin to do some mighty things in your life and in your finances.

Set your priorities.

Deuteronomy 8:18a sets the priority for your finances:

> *But thou shalt remember the LORD thy God: for it is he that giveth thee power to get wealth, (why?)* ***that he***

may establish his covenant . . .

And what is the covenant?

> *And I will make of thee a great nation, and I will bless thee, and make thy name great; (why?) and **thou shalt be a blessing.***
>
> *Genesis 12:2*

Yes, God wants to bless you, so you can go forth and live HIS SECOND PRIORITY: to love and bless your neighbor as you are loved and blessed yourself. God has given you the power to get wealth so that we (the whole Body of Christ) can go forth and preach the Gospel through the entire world without apologizing to anyone, without fussing and fighting over past due bills, and without large extentions of credit.

Yes, God has given us the power to get wealth so we can bring the Gospel to the world, without debts.

Set your priorities.

Go boldly beyond being blessed into being a blessing. You cannot be a blessing to others until you personally have been blessed by God. Surely, now it is time for the church to violently break out of the poverty cycle. It is time to stop the trickle of financial blessings in your life, and to make some violent breakthroughs that will properly fund your endtime vision of reaching the world with the Word of God.

Remember, along with a knowledge of God's plan for abundance, it takes decisive action.

The farmer must first plant seeds. Sometime in very hard ground, from early morning to late at night, in the hot sun, often without lunch. If he wants a great harvest, he must fight to get seed into the ground.

The same is true in your financial walk. Sometimes seed planting is very hard. Circumstances say "You cannot afford to give $50."

But you do it.

Circumstances say "You cannot afford to tithe before you pay your bills."

But you do it.

Circumstances say "You cannot afford to give a specific love gift to your pastor and the offering God has instructed for you to send to some special ministry.

But you do it.

Breakthroughs in sowing (giving) always go before break-

throughs in harvest (receiving).

Remember Galatians 6:9:

And let us not be weary in well doing: for in due season we shall reap (receive), if we faint not.

SECTION NINE:
GOD'S GIFT-GIVING EXAMPLE

Lesson 61: The gift of salvation

If we are to become proper givers, then our giving must be patterned after the greatest gift-giver of all, God, our Heavenly Father. He freely gave us the greatest gift of all, the gift of everlasting life.

*For by grace are ye saved through faith; and that not of yourselves: it is **the gift of God**:*
Not of works, lest any man should boast.

Ephesians 2: 8,9

God gives you SALVATION, through faith, as a free gift! You cannot "earn" your salvation through good works; it is a miracle gift from God.

When God sent Jesus Christ to this earth, Jesus was a free gift, sent to provide us with salvation and eternal life.

O wretched man that I am! Who shall deliver me from the body of this death?
I thank God through Jesus Christ our Lord.

Romans 7:24,25a

For God so loved the world that HE GAVE His only begotten Son, that whoever believes in Him should not perish but have everlasting life.
For God did not send His Son into the world to condemn the world, but that the world through Him might be saved.

John 3:16,17 NKJ

The only thing you can do to receive your free gift of salvation is to simply tell the Lord, "Yes Father, I do accept Jesus into my heart as the Lord and Savior of my life."

Child of God, do you see how totally free the gift of salvation is for you? You can only **accept** the gift; there is absolutely nothing you can do in your own strength to ever earn it!

Always remember this principle whenever you give: Realize the recipient of your gift may have partially earned the gift by good conduct, some work he or she did for you, a ministry that blessed, or a donor gift you wanted. There is nothing wrong with this, but remember this kind of giving, while scriptural, is not of the same quality of motivation as the gift of your salvation.

I recommend you include in your giving not only those who have blessed you, but some who have done absolutely nothing to earn or deserve your gift: The poor. The hungry. A ministry that doesn't even know you are alive. Just send them an offering because you know God wants you to be a giver.

Lesson 62: The gift of faith

In the last lesson, from the second chapter of Ephesians, we learned that God freely saves us, and that salvation comes through THE GIFT of faith. Actually, our faith is a free gift too.

For by grace are ye saved through faith; and that not of yourselves: it is the gift of God:
Not of works, lest any man should boast.

Ephesians 2:8,9

Faith is a critical part of our walk with God.

*But without faith it is **IMPOSSIBLE TO PLEASE HIM:** for he that cometh to God must believe that he is, and that he is a rewarder of them that diligently seek him.*

Hebrews 11:6

But where does our faith come from?

*Looking unto Jesus the **author** and finisher of our faith; who for the joy that was set before him endured the cross, despising the shame, and is set down at the right hand of the throne of God.*

Hebrews 12:2

God freely gave us Jesus Christ, and eternal salvation. And, we can please God, and defeat the enemy in our day-to-day battles with our various circumstances, He freely gave us FAITH. This gift of faith is vital if you are to break out of the bonds of insufficiency that so many Christians languish in this very day. This God-given FAITH is a major key to your financial freedom.

Faith is a major ingredient in attaining the inheritance God has for you.

That ye be not slothful, but followers of them who through faith and patience inherit the promises.

Hebrews 6:12

The promises of God (the abundant supply) are greatly dependent on faith. Guard your faith. Thank God for it, and give it plenty of exercise. As you give, believe in faith that you will receive more

110

and more so that you can give away more and more fruit from your harvest.

> *For God, who gives seed to the farmer to plant, and later on, good crops to harvest and eat, will give you more and more seed to plant and will make it grow so that you can give away more and more fruit from your harvest.*
>
> *2 Corinthians 9:10 TLB*

Yes, God will give you much so that you can give away much.

Lesson 63: The gift of the Holy Spirit

When the Holy Spirit enters your life, God promises many marvelous things will happen:

1. You will receive POWER, and will be a WITNESS:

> *But ye shall receive POWER, after that the Holy Ghost is come upon you: and ye shall be WIT-NESSES unto me both in Jerusalem, and in all Judea, and in Samaria, and unto the uttermost part of the earth.*
>
> *Acts 1:8*

2. Through the Holy Spirit, and the wonderful prayer language He gives you, you can build up your free gift of faith:

> *But ye, beloved, building up yourselves on your most holy faith, praying in the Holy Ghost,*
>
> *Jude 20*

3. When you receive the Holy Spirit, He intercedes for you before the throne of God, for your sicknesses and petitions, in accordance with God's will:

> *Likewise the Spirit also helpeth our infirmities, for we know not what we should pray for as we ought: but the Spirit itself maketh intercession for us with groanings which cannot be uttered.*
>
> *Romans 8:26*

Now, here's the true miracle of the Holy Spirit: God gives His Holy Spirit to us freely. ALL YOU HAVE TO DO **IS ASK** TO RECEIVE!

> *If ye then, being evil, know how to give good gifts unto
> your children: how much more shall your heavenly
> Father give the Holy Spirit to them that ask him?*
>
> *Luke 11:13*

Once you FREELY RECEIVE THE HOLY SPIRIT by asking, then God also bestows upon you the fruits of the Spirit:

> *But the fruit of the Spirit is love, joy, peace, long-
> suffering, gentleness, goodness, faith, meekness, tem-
> perance: against such there is no law.*
>
> *Galatians 5:22,23*

Child of God, are you beginning to grasp what a grand giver God is? He freely gives to you all those things you need to live well in this life, and also in eternity!

This series of lessons on giving are not taking you away from God, but they are bringing you more into His likeness and image:

> *While we look not at the things which are seen, but at
> the things which are not seen; for the things which are
> seen are temporal; but the things which are not seen
> are eternal.*
>
> *2 Corinthians 4:18*

I believe now, at the close of lesson 63, you are getting the breakthrough. If we are sons of God, bone of His bone and flesh of His flesh, then we should show His personality to the world. God is a great giver and we must be like Him, GREAT GIVERS.

Lesson 64: God gives freely and joyfully!

Our great-giving God is continuously giving to us all things that pertain to life and godliness:

> *According as his divine power hath given unto us **all
> things that pertain unto life and godliness,**
> through the knowledge of him that hath called us to
> glory and virtue:*
>
> *2 Peter 1: 3*

Many things pertain unto life: just think of all the things this encompasses. Gasoline for your car is something pertaining to life. Although it seems the price of gasoline is only going up, God knows you need gasoline, and the Bible guarantees that your God will supply "all things that pertain unto life," including groceries, clothes, housing, and jobs. No matter how high the price of groceries, clothes or gasoline goes, it does not matter. Our God promises to supply every need in your life.

Child of God, by now this simple truth must be sinking into your spirit: God wants to bless us so wonderfully, so completely, so powerfully, because He wants you to become a great giver LIKE He is! God wants you to abundantly receive so you can abundantly give.

He wants to position you for the greater blessings He will bring you, for He said it is more blessed to give than to receive.

As you learn to give in your everyday life, you are unleashing the process that will make you more like God. He is the greatest giver, and He wants you to become like Him.

> *Herein is our love made perfect, that we may have boldness in the day of judgment: because **as he is, so are we in this world.***
>
> *1 John 4: 17*

God sees us as He is, so are we, in this world. Can you lay hold of that thought and grasp its eternal significance?

God sees us as He is, in this world, manifesting a walking, talking, proof-producing ministry that brings forth a duplication of Christ on the earth. Isn't it wonderful to think that one day soon your prosperity will grow through your giving to the point that you can truthfully say to all men that meet you:

"I am come that you might have life (you will be ready to lead them into eternal life) and that you can have it more abundantly," (you will be ready to bless them in their needs).

Truly, you are at the threshold of moving beyond receiving the blessing into actually being a blessing.

> *All scripture is given by inspiration of God, and is profitable for doctrine, for reproof, for correction, for instruction in righteousness:*
> *That the man of God man be perfect, **thoroughly furnished unto all good works**.*
>
> *2 Timothy 3:16,17*

Lesson 65: Jesus is a great giver

When God's first son, Jesus Christ, took on the whole nature and personality of His Heavenly Father, He too was a great giver. Hear what the Word says about Jesus:

> *Wherefore he saith, When he ascended up on high, he led captivity captive, **and gave gifts unto men.***
>
> *Ephesians 4:8*

Aren't you glad that the precious recorded words of Jesus are faithfully preserved by the Holy Spirit, and they so clearly tell why He personally came down to this earth: hear Him as He spoke to those that heard those words many years ago:

> *I am come that they might have life, and that they might have it (their new lives) more abundantly.*
>
>

John 10:10b

"I am come that they might have."

Jesus did not come down to earth to make us give up good things and lead a life of sorrow, poverty, and depression. If you read the words of the Lord and His apostles and prophets carefully, you will find that the true intention of God was not to remove us from the world and its possessions, but to actually have us take over this world and its possessions.

By now, you are easily seeing that Jesus came so that this could happen soon.

> *Beloved, I wish above all things that thou mayest prosper and be in health, even as thy soul prospereth.*
>
>

3 John 2

If we are going to function as Jesus functioned, then we must be concerned about more than just our own abundance; we must also be concerned about our brothers and sisters around the world and if they have all that they need. This is not our choice, it is a command:

> **Give to him that asketh thee,** *and from him that would borrow of thee turn not thou away.*
>
>

Matthew 5:42

How will we do this if we are broke and in want ourselves? How can you give to everyone that asks of you? Jesus did. He knew His Heavenly Father would supply everything He needed. He came to give, He literally tapped into the unlimited supply.

And He tells us to walk in the same footsteps.

Jesus told us:

> *Heal the sick, cleanse the lepers, raise the dead, cast out devils:* **freely ye have received, freely give.**
>
>

Matthew 10:8

In freely giving, you open the storehouses of God, and you unleash an unending supply.

Hear the word. Jesus wants you and I to alleviate pain and misery, sorrow, death, disease, sickness – all over the world! Jesus wants us to generously give, out of His unending supply of health and power. He wants our giving to go beyond salvation, health, and deliverance. He wants us to give to the poor. Give water to the thirsty. Give alms to those in need. The scriptures that deal with these benevolent gifts are too numerous to mention here. I know that with each lesson in this last third of our study, you are growing more confident that your decision to imitate Jesus in the grace of giving was one of the best ones you have ever made.

This new grace many times doesn't even require financial resources. You can give peace to the depressed, joy to the unhappy, salvation to the lost, confidence to the inhibited, and yes, you are even now leaving the realm of just the intangible and are becoming a giver of the tangible.

Even if you haven't given $10,000 yet, you are changing your lifestyle from a consumer to a provider. You are literally beginning to come forth in a measure of the stature of Christ. Say this aloud now:

> "My Lord Jesus came that men might have life more abundantly, and as His servant, **I am now here that men might have life more abundantly**."

Lesson 66: The Holy Spirit is a great giver

We have seen that God is a great giver, and that Jesus is a great giver. So, it must spiritually follow that the Holy Spirit is also a great giver.

And the Word of God clearly shows that this is so.

Every informed Christian knows that when you submit yourselves to the Holy Spirit, the Holy Spirit immediately becomes an abundant source of priceless treasures:

> *But the fruit of the Spirit is love, joy, peace, longsuffering, gentleness, goodness, faith, meekness, temperance:*

> *Galatians 5:22,23*

And the list of the fruits of the Spirit goes on:

> *Wisdom, knowledge, faith, healing, miracles, prophecy, distinguishing between Spirit, different kinds of tongues, interpretation of tongues.*

All of these gifts are documented in 1 Corinthians 12: 1-11. The treasure chest of the Holy Spirit is not understandable by sense knowledge, you must catch the depth of the riches.

> *Eye hath not seen, nor ear heard, neither have entered into the heart of man the things which God*

115

hath prepared for them that love Him, but God hath
revealed them unto us by his Spirit:

1 Corinthians 2:9b,10a

And there's still more. The very POWER TO WITNESS is a
free gift of the Holy Spirit:

After they had prayed, the place where they were
assembled together was shaken; and they were all
filled with the Holy Spirit, and they **spoke the word**
of God with boldness.

Acts 4:31 NKJ

Are you beginning to see how much God has in His everlasting,
abundant, inexhaustible storehouse? He has so much for you that
there is literally no place on earth that can contain all of the physical
and spiritual blessings of **God**, the Father; **Jesus**, the Son; and the
Holy Spirit of God.

Remember, the gifts that the Holy Spirit has for you are
infinitely more valuable than all worldly treasures. If you neglected
them and went after material treasures alone, you would do eternal
damage to yourself.

Simon, the sorcerer, whose story is found in Acts 8:14-24, tried
to put a money value on the gifts of the Holy Ghost. He was cursed,
and his money with him, because he lacked a full understanding of
the superior value of the Spirit's gifts, and that brought a curse on
him **and upon his money**. Now attain earthly treasure, but pursue
above all else the gifts of the Spirit, for they are eternal.

Lesson 67: A gift will always prosper the giver

Now that you have refreshed your mind with the knowledge of
our great God's spirit of giving, you can more easily understand
that the world's ways are not God's ways. Surely, the biblical
principles in this section have amplified that point.

By the world's principles of economics, when you give something away, you then have less. If you give away money or land or
food, that leaves you with less of the thing you have given away.

But such is not the case according to God's principles of economics. He teaches that when you give something away, it **always**
ends up returning to you, **multiplied**.

In God's economy, any gift you give away **always** ends up
prospering you beyond the point you were at when you gave the gift
in the first place. Simply stated, you cannot loose ground by giving
to God.

116

In God's principles of economics, when you give a gift, you release His energy into your own life to duplicate the gift in multiplied quantity. Gifts become very powerful things that reach beyond the natural realm into the Spirit realm and increase themselves, some thirty-fold, some sixty-fold, and some one-hundred-fold.

> *A gift is as a precious stone in the eyes of him that hath it: whithersoever it turneth, it prospereth.*
>
> *Proverbs 17:8*

When you give a gift to a person, and even if they throw it away, it doesn't stop the spiritual energy of that gift from working towards **prospering your life**. Even if the gift is misued, that gift will begin to prosper you.

Notice, God says He will prosper the giver, not the gift.

The world says the gift depletes your wealth. **Logic says** when you give something away, you no longer have it. But, God's Word says that a gift does not deplete your assets, it INCREASES them!

Every gift you give becomes an invisible miracle force that draws more of whatever you have given away, right back to you. That is a powerful concept.

Look now at another marvelous promise God makes to the giver:

> *Many will entreat the favor of the prince: and **every man is a friend to him that giveth gifts**.*
>
> *Proverbs 19:6*

When you give gifts, it shows that you are willing to meet the needs of others. Because of this generous nature, the Bible teaches you will have friends. Your gift will not "buy" their friendship, but your heart, your generous nature will supernaturally attract people to you with well-being in their hearts.

The dimension of this supernatural power that is released by the God-motivated giver even reaches into the camp of your enemies. When we obey God in every aspect of our lives, which includes giving as He directs us, He becomes very pleased with us, and even our enemies are caught up in a new attitude towards us.

> *When a man's ways please the Lord, he maketh even his enemies to be at peace with him.*
>
> *Proverbs 16:7*

Your gift is a natural key that unleashes a supernatural miracle working force in your life.

You may say: "Well, Brother John, I just don't believe that."

Friend, it does not make any difference whether you believe it or not. The Bible says it, and that's a fact. God wants you to have friends, and He promises friends as one of the rewards for being a gracious giver.

Lesson 68: God's giving guarantee

We have seen that giving is a gift of God. It is "godlike" and draws us closer to His Image. We learned that it will make you prosperous, and that it releases supernatural miracle-working power in and around your life.

Now, I want you to realize that this entire process is completely guaranteed! It is a spiritual law, as powerful and as dependable as any natural law.

> *Give, and it shall be given unto you; good measure, pressed down, and shaken together, and running over, shall men give into your bosom. For with the same measure that ye (measure), it shall be measured to you again.*
>
> *Luke 6:38*
>
> *Be not deceived; God is not mocked: for whatsoever a man soweth, that shall he also reap.*
>
> *Galatians 6:7*

So often, when the offering plate is passed in church, or a ministry asks for your support, a question goes through your mind: "I wonder if I can afford to give?"

Well, Child of God, you are asking the wrong question. The question you should be asking yourself is: **"Can I afford NOT to give?"**

You see, God has guaranteed that the gift always comes back, in good measure, pressed down, shaken together, and running over. Whatever you sow you will reap.

That is certainly better than Wall Street can promise you! That's better than the interest at your local savings and loan! The Bible says men will give unto your bosom (notice, it does not just say the saints will give to you, it simply says "men"). Today, there are more than 4.8 billion people on the world – that's how many instruments God has available to bless you.

That's God's promise: When you give to the things of God, you can trust God to give back to you.

118

Once again, this process of returning the gift to you is not just left to chance, it is a guaranteed rate of return: It comes back to you **in the same measure that you gave**. If you give a thimble full, you will get back many thimbles full. If you give a teaspoon full, you will get back teaspoons of blessing. But, if you upgrade and start giving shovels full, look out, because God must move up to shovel's full.

And do not be afraid if you want to move into the big league of giving. God has truckloads for those who give by the truck. You see, He promises the same measure. Give a little, and you shall get a little. Give a lot, and God will overwhelm you with His blessings in return.

> *But remember this – if you give little, you will get little.*
>
> *A farmer who plants just a few seeds will get only a small crop, but if he plants much, he will reap much.*
>
> 2 Corinthians 9: 6 TLB

Lesson 69: You can afford a gift

You believed God for your salvation – and got it.

You believed God for your healing – and got it.

You believed God when you asked for the Holy Spirit – and got it.

Now, surely, you can can believe God in gift-giving. When you do, I believe we will see something similar to the time of Moses when the giving was so generous that Moses actually commanded:

> *Let neither man nor woman make any more work for the offering of the sanctuary. So the people were restrained from bringing.*
>
> *For the stuff they had* **was sufficient for all the work to make it, and too much.**
>
> Exodus 36: 6b, 7

Every mission outreach could have more than enough. Every Christian television program could have more than enough. Every church expansion program, every Sunday school auditorium, every Christian camp could have more than enough. Every home in the world could have a Christian worker knocking at the door, inviting them to become a child of God, and offering to meet their family needs, no matter what they are.

What a miracle day that would be! But for it to happen, you and I and those others that are being enlightened to the principles of

119

Biblical economics must press into dimensions of giving and receiving that will release such a floodtide of abundance into the gospel ministry that Satan's lie of insufficiency will be rendered powerless. And, as our brethren lay hold upon this truth in mass numbers, they will erradicate hunger, want, and insufficiency from our planet.

Our giving can usher in a new day of plenty in a new Kingdom of God here on earth.

ALL OF ISRAEL was involved in giving, that's why Moses had to command the people to stop. There simply was too much. Call us dreamers, if you must, but the truth of God relating to abundance will come to pass. **The reapers will literally overtake the sowers.**

Lesson 70: There's more than enough

God is building a church to be His special dwelling place in these last days. There is a world out there to reach, and God wants to reach it. But, if you are continuously sitting around trying to figure out how much you want to give to God, you will probably talk yourself out of 90 percent of what God intended you to give SO THAT HE CAN REALLY BLESS YOU!

Child of God, hold this truth in your spirit: your King of Kings, your Lord of Lords **is not low on funds**! He isn't about to go bankrupt, but He is trying to keep you from getting low on funds or going bankrupt. We know that when the federal government runs out of money, they just print more of it. But it is against the law for us to print money. So, God has devised this wonderful plan for replenishing our treasury.

He doesn't need printing presses to produce money for His children. He uses a superior method to instruct us in the supernatural realm of creating what we need.

Yes, miracle power awaits you if you dare to apply God's method of obtaining. You know God obtains; He does it by giving.

*For God so loved the world, that **he gave** his only begotten Son, that whosoever believeth in him should not perish, but have everlasting life.*

John 3:16

When God wanted sons, He gave His Son; now He has millions of sons.

This principle worked for the lady of Zarephath. There was more than enough for her when SHE GAVE to the prophet Elijah.

120

There was more than enough for Moses when he called upon his people to bring offerings to the sanctuary.

There was more than enough when Jesus had to feed the multitudes with five loaves and two fishes.

And there is more than enough for your life!

Do you **honestly believe** that you could give **more** to God than God could give back to you? Can you really ever imagine God watching you give, and then saying: "Ooops, that did it. You just gave me more than my current supply of blessings. There's no possible way I can ever give THAT MUCH back to you." Do you really think that you could break the bank of heaven?

Absolutely not. It will never happen.

Remember, I told you Moses had "too much" because the saints of God in his day grasped this spiritual concept. Well, just read one bit of the description concerning the sanctuary they were building:

> *And he overlaid the boards with gold, and made their rings of gold to be places for the bars, and overlaid the bars with gold.*

> *Exodus 36:34*

Notice when the abundance of God is envisioned and acted upon there is no need for scrimping.

Child of God, realize it; visualize it; verbalize it.

There is more than enough for you!

GOD'S GIFT-GIVING EXAMPLE

IN SUMMARY

All well-informed Christians understand that they are made in the **image and likeness** of God. However, sometimes we fail to grasp exactly what is that image and likeness.

God is a giver. Jesus Christ is a giver. The **Holy Spirit** is a giver. If you are to live in the measure of the image and likeness of God, you must become a **great giver**.

Some of you are currently giving tiny eyedropper-sized gifts, God desires more for your life. Eyedropper-sized blessings will not sustain you in these endtimes.

You need to go beyond giving the minimum to giving the maximum. To get that kind of a breakthrough, you will have to become violent.

When you first were saved, you strongly and aggressively

defeated the forces of evil that came against you. You were told by your neighbors, friends, and sometimes even family that you were not the way you used to be.

Praise God!

If you would have continued in a passive posture, you would never have received your salvation breakthrough; you would have undoubtedly gone back to your old life. You remember you had to bring forth a violent defense in the spirit world to win the victory over the devil.

When you first heard about healing, you had to abandon your false beliefs that healing is not for our day. It took strong faith to lay hands on someone the first time and pray for their healing.

You did not want to do it. It was not comfortable. But you went ahead, and violently pressed back the negative forces, and God brought the healing.

The first time you heard about the Holy Spirit and the possibility of you speaking in new tongues, it felt awkward. No passive effort would have taken you into that BREAKTHROUGH of receiving the Holy Spirit. You had to violently break away from your misconceptions and open your mouth and speak forth those wonderful new utterances that were forming in your mind.

And now, today, you are in the process of another major SPIRITUAL BREAKTHROUGH – a fantastic, supernatural financial breakthrough. Even now it is stirring in the heavenly realm around you.

But, it will not come to full manifestation without a violent, forceful effort on your part.

The next time the offering basket comes to you in church, Satan will try and rob you of the breakthrough victory. "You can't afford to give," he will try to tell you. "You haven't paid the rent yet. You have already given quite a bit."

Child of God, this is not your subconscious mind talking; it is the enemy. He wants to rob you and see you destitute.

Violently attack him by saying: "Get behind me, Satan. Get out of this matter. It is none of your business. All of my substance, my money, my equity, and my potential income is already dedicated to Jesus Christ, my Lord and Savior. I dedicated it to Him, and it shall be used to spread the Gospel around the world as He leads me to give. AND, now I stand on GOD'S PROMISE that He will return everything to me I give to Him in even greater proportion than I gave, so that I can give even more the next time"!

When the offering basket comes to you, don't just throw your money in. Take time to pray over your money, **dedicate** it to the Lord, and then put it into the basket with confidence, knowing the return is guaranteed by God. The simple act of putting your money in the basket is a spiritual step which releases God's miracle-working power into your financial life.

There are three steps you should take when giving your money to God:

1. **Decide** it (how much is God saying to give).
2. **Dedicate** it (set it apart as holy money, dedicated to God).
3. **Deposit** it (release it at your earliest convenience).

You are now well into the financial breakthrough you have desired for so long! Always remember to give a bit beyond your comfort zone. Don't ever give only what you can afford. Remember, you are not sacrificially giving out of your great need, you are literally giving your way to financial prosperity.

Take the devil to the woodshed with your next offering! Put him in his place under your feet by your giving.

Even now the abundance of God is moving upon you.

> *And all these blessings shall come on thee, and over-take thee, if thou shalt hearken unto the voice of the Lord thy God.*
>
> *Deuteronomy 28:2*

SECTION TEN:
FIVE KINDS OF GIVING

Lesson 71: The tithe . . . is it still necessary?

There is probably more confusion in the Body of Christ about tithing than any other single type of giving. But God is not the author of confusion, and His Word **is clear** on the tithe.

> *Will a man rob God? Yet ye have robbed me. But ye say, wherein have we robbed thee?* **In tithes and offerings.**
>
> *Ye are cursed with a curse: for ye have robbed me, even this whole nation.*
>
> *Bring ye all the tithes into the storehouse, that there may be food in mine house, and prove me now herewith, saith the Lord of hosts, if I will not open (for) you the windows of heaven, and pour you out for you a blessing, that there shall not be room enough to receive it.*
>
> *Malachi 3:8-10*

If you are going to receive the optimum God-kind of prosperity in your life, you must not overlook or underemphasize the basic building blocks of your Biblical prosperity plan. It is absolutely necessary for you to be following the Biblical plan in the area of tithing. To get the windows of heaven open — and keep them open — you must tithe. **It is not a Biblical option**. It is something you literally owe to God.

"Well, Brother John, that sure takes the spirituality out of giving," you might be saying. "You make it sound like MY TITHE IS AN OBLIGATION, and **not a free act of my will to give.**"

Please remember, these are not my thoughts. God says if you do not tithe, you are committing robbery. He says you owe the tithe to Him. There is one important distinction: your **tithe** is given, not at your discretion, but **because God commands it**. By faithfully bringing forth the tithe to Him, you establish your basic honesty and obedience (see at your leisure Leviticus 27:30-33. It clearly shows that the tithe belongs to the Lord).

However, your offerings are given out of your own generosity. They are totally at your own discretion, and they establish the level of your concern for the things of God.

Every one must make up his own mind as to how
much he should give. Don't force anyone to give more
than he really wants to, for cheerful givers are the
ones God prizes. God is able to make it up to you by
giving you everything you need and more, so that
there will not only be enough for your own needs, but
plenty left over to give joyfully to others.

2 Corinthians 9:7 TLB

Remember, you are not being generous when you tithe. You are simply obeying God. **Tithing is not an option**.

In Hebrews 7: 1-10, we see that Abraham paid the tithes. He paid them for himself, **before** the dispensation of the Law, and also paid them for Levi, who lived under the dispensation of grace. Abraham also tithed for all posterity – for his natural children (seed), and for the spiritual children (seed) who now live in the dispensation of grace.

And if ye be Christ's, then are ye Abraham's seed, and
heirs according to the promise.

Galatians 3:29

The obligation of tithing reaches across the pre-law dispensations, the dispensation of the law, and now, into the post-law dispensation of grace.

Remember, the windows of heaven are opened by the faithful giving of your tithes, making this basic giving (the tithe) absolutely necessary. For, without the windows of heaven open, nothing can flow from God to you.

Lesson 72: Where should the tithe be given?

There is great controversy as to where your tithe should be given. Some say it should go to your local church. Others say Bible colleges should receive it. Still others want the tithe to go strictly for world evangelism.

What I understand to be the biblical answer is found in the third chapter of Malachi. There we see that the tithe goes into "**the storehouse**." The context says that this storehouse is the place where the meat (Word) is kept and supplied to the saints.

Bring ye all the tithes into the storehouse, that there
may be meat in mine house, and prove me now here-
with, saith the Lord of hosts, if I will not open you the

windows of heaven, and pour you out a blessing, that
there shall not be room enough to receive it.

Malachi 3:10

Where are you being fed the unadulterated Word of God? This is the question you must answer to determine where to give your tithe. The place you are being spiritually fed should be your local church, and above every other place, that is where you should tithe.

But, the truth of the matter is that there are not enough local churches truly reaching into every level of society to make this a hard and fast tithing rule. Many saints are sick and unable to journey to church. Perhaps some of these saints receive their spiritual meat from a Christian television or radio program, or a good ministry to shut-ins. Surely this is an exception to the general answer.

Now, some local pastors may not agree with this, but I must be faithful to the convictions God gives me from His word, and believe they will not let this tithing teaching cause a division between us. I understand the necessity for the tithe to go into good local churches because for over eighteen years I pastored local churches, and I instructed my congregation that if they were receiving their spiritual meat from another storehouse, that is where their tithe should go.

I never in all of my pastorate had any trouble with any reasonable saint of God in failing to tithe to our church. I found that the best way to insure the tithe would come to our church was to be sure that our church was always full of good strong meat (the rightly divided Word of God).

Notice another aspect of this verse: God says to tithe, and "prove me." God is literally challenging you to put Him to the test in this matter of tithing. He wants the windows of heaven to be open in your life. There is no other place in scripture that I know of where God so clearly challenges us to test Him and His Word. Child of God, it must be becoming wonderfully clear that He **wants only to bless you!** But, He cannot do it through closed windows.

Let's keep up our momentum. We know we must tithe, and why, and now according to the Word of God where we should tithe. So, let's keep putting God to the test by consistently tithing, and we will see the windows of heaven open in our lives.

Remember: The tithe goes to the place where you receive your spiritual meat on a consistent basis. For most of us, it is our full gospel church. If, however, you are in a church that does not preach the entire Word of God, go before God and prayerfully ask Him to lead you to the church near you that will systematically and faithfully feed you the meat of God's Word.

Lesson 73: Can there be prosperity without the tithe?

God wants to build an endtime temple – a holy habitation of God, not made with hands – but to do this He must have a great endtime army of very special saints to accomplish it. That's not just a fancy idea, but it came to me by revelation after twenty-nine years of studying the Holy Bible. It's totally based upon Scripture.

God will give the responsibility of building this great endtime dwelling place to those who are proven faithful in financial matters.

When King Josiah commissioned workers for the restoration of the temple he gave the work to those craftsmen who already had proven themselves FAITHFUL in their **financial transactions.**

> *To repair the breaches of the house, unto carpenters, and builders, and masons, and to buy timber and hewn stone to repair the house. Howbeit **there was no reckoning made with them of the money that was delivered into their hand, because they dealt faithfully.***
>
> *2 Kings 22: 5c-7*

These men were not chosen to partake in this labor because they PROMISED to be faithful, but they were chosen because they had **already** proven themselves to be faithful! When it came time for King Josiah to choose who would work in the great restoration of the temple, God told the king to choose these men because they had an established record of **dealing faithfully in their finances**.

God uses people who are faithful in their finances, and tithing is part of that faithfulness.

I've heard many people throughout the world tell me: "Oh Brother John, when I get a large sum of money (such as an inheritance or sweepstakes winning, or some get rich quick scheme), then I will become a faithful giver to things of God."

That is not God's way!

First, God **requires** that you are faithful in the little matters, right where you are, in the midst of your present circumstances, and then afterwards God will grant you an abundance.

That was true in the Old and New Testaments, and it is true today. In the parable of the talents, what did the ruler say to his faithful servant?

His lord said unto him, Well done, good and faithful
servant; **thou hast been faithful over a few things,**
I will make thee ruler over many things: *Enter*
thou into the joy of thy lord.

Matthew 25:23

And:

He that is faithful in that which is least is faithful
also in much: and he that is unjust in the least is
unjust also in much.

Luke 16:10

If you want to be a part of the next big move of God, don't just get your finances in order temporarily, keep them in order from now on.

Remember, 1 Corinthians 4:2:

Moreover, it is required (not just desired) in stew-
ards, that a man be found faithful.

1 Corinthians 4:2

Lesson 74: What is an offering?

I am sure by now you have realized your offering is greatly different than your tithe. The tithe is clearly ten percent of what you earn, an amount set by God which is paid to Him as a debt, or a non-negotiable obligation that you owe to Him. Failure to pay the tithe is plainly called robbery in God's Word.

I know that is frank and to the point, but there is no sense in beating around the bush with God's Word. He says it, so what can we do other than just believe it, abandon all debate?

But offerings – now that's a different matter!

An offering is not a specified amount; it is totally discretionary on your part, an amount you freely give to God to establish a rate of return from Him that is **acceptable** or **desirable to you**. By the amount of your offering the measure or rate by which God will bless you and increase your substance is established:

For with the same measure that ye (measure) it shall
be measured to you again.

Luke 6:38

An offering is anything you give – over and above your tithe. You are not a generous giver in the eyes of God when you tithe – the tithe is simply being honest and giving God what you "owe" Him.

But, when you hear the voice of God leading you to help finance a struggling ministry in the Philippines, or as you obey the Holy Spirit when He tells you to send $50 to a ministry fighting drug abuse in a certain city, now that is an offering, a FREEWILL LOVE OFFERING TO YOUR GOD!

Who is going to tithe to a Christian home for abused children? The only people receiving "meat" from this "spiritual storehouse" would be the little abused children in the home – and they do not have the finances to support the home. So this home, and many more projects in God's Kingdom survive solely through the freewill offerings of God's prosperous people!

Remember, the principles of biblical economics only start when we tithe. They are set in motion when we give generous offerings. There is a great blessing in the offerings, because the offering determines the measure God uses to give back to us. And, the offering is always a blessing to the ministries receiving them, since in many cases these offerings are God's way of meeting their needs.

Through your tithes and offerings you will move into a dynamic new realm as a mature Christian, working with God, ministering to the needs of a hurting and needy world.

> *And they went forth, and preached everywhere, the*
> *Lord working with them, and confirming the word*
> *with signs following. Amen.*
>
> > *Mark 16:20*

Lesson 75: The hidden blessing of giving to world missions

When you seriously search God's Word, you discover there is a spiritual gift of giving, and that spiritual gift has many different manifestations. One is the releasing of the tithe. Another is the giving of an offering. In this lesson, we will talk about a third type of giving: specific giving to world missions.

There is a **very special type of blessing** God gives to those who support world missions. Read this key verse in its context:

> *Now ye Philippians know also that in the beginning*
> *of the gospel, when I departed from Macedonia (on a*
> *great mission journey), no church (shared) with me*
> *as concerning giving and receiving, but ye only.*
> *For even in Thessalonia (one of the mission fields) ye*
> *sent once and again unto my necessity.*

Not because I desire a gift: but I desire fruit that may abound to your account.

But my God shall supply all your need according to his riches in glory by Christ Jesus.
Philippians 4:15-17 & 19

The last verse of this scripture is continuously quoted, out of context, by well-meaning but uninformed Christians everywhere. They are claiming Philippians 4:19 because it sounds desirable, but read the entire passage in its God-given context. This promise is not intended for just every Christian; it is given to a very exclusive group: those who faithfully support world missions.

The context here shows that God will supply all the needs of those who are as the Philippians were – giving to world missions. But notice God did not say He would supply their needs **out of** His riches in glory, but He clearly states that He will supply their needs **according** to His riches in glory.

Now, let him that has an ear hear what the spirit of God is saying: (This won't make sense to most, but it will witness to those who are catching a vision of the mind of God.)

The promise reads, "But my God shall supply all your need according to his riches in glory." The word "according" speaks of God's blessing upon those who give to missions in the same **quality, not quantity**, as His own riches in glory!

God provides a way for you to have both abundance, and to have quality. Right now, all evil imaginations are trying to arise and find fault with this statement.

Remember, Our Lord Jesus Christ is the one who freely gave the best wine to His friends at the marriage supper. He also encouraged costly oil to be poured over Him. And, when He was crucified, His coat was of the very best kind, causing the soldiers to cast lots for it. In the book of Revelation, in chapter one He is seen among the golden candlesticks wearing a solid gold girdle.

God will supply the needs of His faithful partners in evangelizing the world, **in accordance with His riches in glory**!

Lesson 76: Scripturally giving to your teacher

Every Christian has some special teacher who is vital in their Christian life. There are prophecy teachers, Bible teachers, pastors, evangelists, and those who, like myself, instruct you in the financial matters of the Word.

There is a continuous flow of good teaching available to us each day, but did you know that the Bible tells us if we are receiving a blessing from a teacher, then we should share good things with that teacher?

> Let him that is taught in the word (share with) him
> that teacheth **in all good things**.
>
> Galatians 6:6

I hope by this time in our study, you have learned this; I do not bring this up because I desire a gift from you, but, as Paul, I do desire fruit that will abound to your account!

I am teaching this concept to you because IT IS THE TRUTH, and only as you know the truth can you be set totally free! Galatians 6:6 declares it: God says we should take from our good things and share them with those who teach the Word of God.

What a great plan this is. He gives great anointed teachers to bring you His wonderful word. After you learn the Word, you go forth and benefit and prosper from that Word. Then, you share some of that prosperity with your teacher to help meet his needs and to fulfill God's Word to him which says: "Thou shalt not muzzle the ox when he treadeth out the corn," (Deuteronomy 25:4). God promises the teacher will eat freely from the harvest he planted in your spirit.

When you give to your teacher, you unleash God's prosperity even more powerfully in your life. You have given the Heavenly Father yet another avenue through which He can bless you.

What a wonderful ever-increasing cycle of blessing!

Now look at the very next line of that Scripture:

> Be not deceived, God is not mocked: for whatsoever a
> man soweth, that shall he also reap.
>
> Galatians 6:7

As you sow a blessing TO your teacher, you will reap a blessing FROM your teacher, and grow into an even deeper understanding of God's Word. Bless those who teach you, and God promises He will bless you in return.

Lesson 77: Taking the veil off Malachi 3:10

Because of the importance of this principle, I must re-emphasize it. This is one of the most important lessons in this book because it answers a much-asked question by good-intentioned Christians: "Brother John, I have been faithfully tithing now for

131

ten years, and very frankly, I have never one time received a blessing that there was not room enough to receive it!"

Every tithing Christian probably relates to this dilemma.

Here is why the tithe has not been manifesting the blessings described in Malachi 3:10: most Christians are giving **precisely their 10 percent**, and not a penny more!

When you tithe, you are simply returning to God what is already His. It is not a gift, because if you keep it, you are robbing God! There is even a penalty for using the tithe – God says you owe Him 20 percent interest when you pay it back:

> *And all **the tithe** of the land, whether of the seed of the land, or of the fruit of the tree, **is the Lord's**: it is holy unto the Lord.*
> *And if a man will at all redeem (any) of his tithes, he shall add thereto the fifth part (20 percent) thereof.*
>
> *Leviticus 27: 30,31*

The spiritual principles that govern the blessings of the tithe are contained in Malachi 3:10:

> *Bring ye all the tithes into the storehouse, that there may be meat in mine house, and prove me now herewith, saith the Lord of hosts, if I will not open the windows of heaven, and pour you out a blessing, that **there shall** not **be room** enough **to receive it**.*

I have emphasized seven words in this text that are written in italics in the King James version. It is common knowledge that all italicized words in the King James version have been added by the translators to the original Greek text. Here is one of the few big errors in the translation of the authorized version.

These words, **their shall be room to receive it**, are added words, which do not clarify the original text, as italicized words are supposed to do, but actually add a meaning that God did not intend.

The passage should properly read: "and pour out for you a blessing, **that not enough**."

You see, tithing only opens the windows of heaven. If you had someone living next to you who was stealing from you, you wouldn't leave the windows open.

The same is true of God. When you fail to tithe, you are stealing from Him, and HE SHUTS THE WINDOWS of financial blessings in your life!

But, when we do tithe, He opens the windows of heaven, but remember, the literal meaning of the original text says **that is not enough**. We must then complete the process through offerings to establish the rate of return out of those windows. After we tithe to open the windows, then we put to work Luke 6:38:

The only giving we do is through our offerings, over and above the tithe. These offerings are so critical because they determine how much we receive back from God through the open windows (opened by the tithe).

For with the same measure that ye (measure), it shall be measured to you again.

Luke 6:38b

Remember, your tithe opens the windows of heaven, and your offering establishes the measure of God's giving back to you through the open windows.

FIVE KINDS OF GIVING
IN SUMMARY

If you want nice, simple, easy answers concerning giving and receiving, you will not find them in God's Word. You see, He has created His principles of biblical economics, and they require time, study, and understanding to become effective and POWERFUL in your life. The biblical principles of economics are **not an "instant" prosperity formula**. They demand understanding, AND a new relationship with God.

The gift of your salvation is given freely, but it then takes a constant daily walk to keep your relationship with God growing.

You received the Holy Spirit simply by asking, but if you plan to put all of the gifts and fruits of the Holy Spirit into POWERFUL PRACTICE in your life, it takes a lifetime of interaction with Him.

The same is true of the Biblical principles of giving and receiving.

It is not an instantaneous gift. The principle of giving and receiving demand careful study to understand God's will for you in this matter: they demand faithful execution in a systematic, concise manner. And then, after faith and patience have done their work, we inherit the promises described in Hebrews 6:12.

In this section, you have seen that there are many types of giving.

I listed tithing as one method of giving to God. The tithe is a sum of God's money that has been entrusted to your keeping. Failing to give it back to Him at the proper time is an absolute robbery.

But, the act of tithing is the FOUNDATIONAL PRINCIPLE OF BIBLICAL ECONOMICS since the windows of heaven cannot be opened until you tithe.

You learned that offerings are the key to the measure of your prosperity. Your faithful tithing opens the windows, and your faithful, liberal offerings determine how much God will bless you through the open windows. Giving only a little measure of what you have as an offering brings a little measure of blessing through the windows, but a big measure brings forth a big blessing.

Mission-giving unleashes a very special promise JUST FOR YOU! No other saints can experience prosperity in quite the same way as those who give to missions. The mission-minded saints can look forward to both quantity and quality blessings from God.

Child of God, GIVING IS A SPIRITUAL GIFT, and we learn to use by APPLICATION. It is **not enough** for you to understand everything that I've written and shared with you in this book, and it is **not enough** for you to memorize every single scripture I've quoted so far, and then STAND IN FAITH for your prosperity.

To achieve God's desired prosperity for your life, to achieve the abundance that will give you the ability to effectively participate in the endtime harvest, YOU MUST FAITHFULLY APPLY THESE PRINCIPLES in your everyday life.

1. **Give** your gift in the name of Jesus.
2. **Pray** over your gift, consecrate it to God's service, then
3. **Release** your gift so God can unleash His POWERFUL PRINCIPLES of abundant supply back into your life.

Give consistently. Give when it is not easy to give; give when it is joyous. Give like the little widow lady who threw in her last two mites in desperation. Be instant in season and out of season.

Simply stated, **Just give**.

God looks at your heart, not at the dollar amount of your gift. He determines the size (or measure) of your gift by what portion it is of what you have. If you are giving out of your need, even if it is only one cent, it is very possible that one cent is a gift of more value than another person giving $1 million out of their great abundance!

That is the only way it can be fair, and God is a just God. These principles make no sense to the world, but they make great sense to God, and, they are making more and more sense to you as you receive a whole new mentality on the subject of finances. Your mind is being revolutionized and renovated, and brought into line, precept upon precept, with the Word of God!

SECTION ELEVEN:
WHO IS BEHIND YOUR POVERTY?

Lesson 78: The source of poverty

Many people believe that poverty and prosperity are both matters of birth, or luck. They believe some people are meant to be poor, and others are meant to be rich.

That is not what the Word of God says.

God has established certain **general** principles of economics that govern who will be rich, and who will be poor. These principles pertain to the lost as well as the saved.

Principle 1:   Laziness tends to poverty.

How long wilt thou sleep, O sluggard? when wilt thou arise out of thy sleep?

Yet a little sleep, a little slumber, a little folding of the hands to sleep:

So shall thy poverty come as one that travelleth, and thy want as an armed man.

Proverbs 6:9-11

The Word is saying here that if you are lazy (and sleep a lot), and do not work (but just sit, folding your hands, wasting time), then poverty will overtake you and work its will in your life, with the same ease and surety that a well-armed robber accomplishes the same task in the life of an unarmed traveler. A violation of this principle can stop the whole process of abounding in a Christian's life, even if he works the formula of abundance.

If you are lazy, if you do not work, then do not expect the principles of Biblical economics to work for you. Furthermore, the Word of God guarantees you will be both poor and desperate.

Now lay hold of this truth: God will not violate His own laws. If you are lazy, you will never be able to operate the principles of Biblical economics in this book, because when you put two opposite forces to work in your life, they continously hinder and nullify each other. Remember too, your prosperity cannot come to you in appreciable measure if your laziness is keeping the armed robber of poverty in the midst of your pending harvest.

If you have a tendency towards laziness, you must change it immediately. You must defend yourself against it with the same resolution that you would defend yourself against an armed robber, remembering, amazing as it may seem, you yourself are a big part of your problem.

We all play a great part in determining our own poverty by our actions! And of course, Satan does his part too. He will lie to you in every imaginable way to keep you poor. He will tell you several myths about money, by saying: "Money is evil, you don't need it," or he will whisper, "If you have money, it will corrupt you," or he will suggest, "You will be even poorer if you give to God," and he will declare, "It is a godly thing to be poor."

You see, poverty is a partnership. The devil wants you poor, and he will lie to you to keep you from doing the Biblical things that will result in wealth.

Poverty is a joint venture between ourselves, Satan, and our ignorance of God's Word. Remember, you have control over the armed robber of laziness, so rebuke it, shun it, and do not fall prey to it, for laziness will destroy the good things that God wants for you.

Lesson 79: The source of prosperity

Just as there are certain general principles of economics that lead to poverty, so too there are **general** principles of economics that lead to prosperity.

Principle 2:   If you are **not lazy**, and can do your **work without constant supervision**, then your life will be tending towards prosperity:

> Go to the ant, thou slaggard; consider her ways, and be wise:
> Which **having no guide, overseer, or ruler,**
> Provideth her meat in the summer, and gathereth her food in the harvest.
>
> Proverbs 6:6-8

This is God's formula for having meat in the summer and food during the harvest: Work hard, like the ant, and do your work without requiring constant supervision! This one truth alone is part of every financial success story ever told!

A field trip to the ant hill that the wise man of Proverbs prescribes is absolutely essential. Whenever a hard-working, industrious man or woman puts the specific principles of Biblical Economics to work, all they do will be more effective.

God's Law of Prosperity says if you are a liberal giver, then your money will be increased.

When a person is industrious, he will naturally tend towards prosperity, so be careful not to loose sight of the fact that you are on a quest for the God-kind of prosperity, and it is based upon giving.

> *There is (he) that scattereth, and yet increaseth; and there is (he) that withholdeth more than is (fitting), but it tendeth to poverty.*
> **The liberal soul shall be made fat, and he that watereth shall be watered also himself.**
>
> *Proverbs 11:24,25*

If you put Jesus first in your finances, then YOU WILL STEADILY INCREASE and become well endowed in material goods.

Keep yourself in balance in your economics. Remember, there are **two sets** of economic principles that must be blended into a successful financial endeavor:

One: The **general** law of economics says that hard work by those who can perform their work without supervision tends towards sufficiency.

Two: The **spiritual** law of biblical economics says that when you give to God, He continuously gives back to you in ever-increasing amounts.

When you operate both the **general** and the spiritual laws of prosperity in your life, you will begin to experience ever-increasing abundance.

Lesson 80: Satan exposed . . . and deposed

Satan is a thief. He is a deceptive, calculating plunderer who, if left unchecked and at his own discretion, moves in and out of your life, trying to find ways to defraud and rob you.

He has stolen the joys of family life by selling his destructive doctrine of divorce to millions. He has stolen the joys of sharing with others in our society by selling his "me first" philosophy.

And, he has stolen from the finances of the saints by convincing the Body of Christ that poverty is godly, and that prosperity is an evil matter.

His lies have kept us crippled, ineffective, and impotent long enough! Satan has "ripped off" from God's children the quality of life God has intended for His saints. (To learn more details, you will

137

want to order my book, **Stolen Property Returned**. It gives you a step-by-step biblical process on how to reclaim those things the devil has stolen in your life).

Establish this principle clearly in your mind: God wants me to be prosperous, and the devil wants me poor. God has given you the Biblical Principles of Economics to achieve prosperity, and Satan has ALL THE LIES you need to keep you poor. Prosperity is a MATERIAL state, but it is attained through a SPIRITUAL BATTLE!

> *For we wrestle not against flesh and blood, but against principalities, against powers, against the rulers of the darkness of this world, against spiritual wickedness in high places.*
>
> *Ephesians 6:12*

It is time we expose, and depose, the devil for the father-of-lies that he is! The devil has used his lies about money to destroy good relationships, to break up families, and even to split churches. But hear me. The money wasn't evil, it was **Satan's lies** about money that caused the evil!

It is time to serve notice on the devil! He has robbed you long enough. For too long and in too many situations he has ripped off your possessions, and indiscriminately ripped off the possessions of the saints of God, literally diminishing our quality of life,

It is time to take a stand.

Please realize that while I have only touched on this subject in this lesson, it is very important. You see, if you do not learn how to stop the devil's robberies in your life, no matter how much you prosper, it will seem like no progress if you do not stop the future robberies of your goods by Satan.

You may want to seriously consider ordering my book, **Stolen Property Returned**. It will give you strong Biblical information that will show you how to get back the wealth and valuables that you have previously lost, and it will show how to keep the new wealth that is now flowing through the principle of giving and receiving into your life.

Lesson 81: Recognizing your prosperity heritage

You now know that the devil wants you poor.

You now know that God has given you authority over the devil, and that He, God, wants you abounding in all good things. By now I am sure you have abandoned the old, worn out God-is-putting-me-through-this-poverty-to-keep-me-dependent-upon-Him story.

Put that kind of thinking in the garbage can.

We are no longer talking old pie-in-the-sky, sweet-by-and-by rhetoric. We are replacing it with scriptural promises of our divine right to be prosperous. Prosperity is part of our **heavenly heritage** that comes with being a child of the King!

With your new prosperity mentality, you are literally being transformed into a new breed of saint. You have a way to put the crooked things straight, the ability to take back what the devil has stolen, and you have a way to bring forth a significant portion of the riches to finance the final, endtime harvest before Jesus comes!

One passage of scripture puts your position in this SPIR-ITUAL BATTLE and SPIRITUAL HERITAGE into proper perspective better than any other:

> *Behold, I GIVE UNTO YOU POWER to tread on serpents and scorpions, and over ALL THE POWER of the enemy: and nothing shall by any means hurt you.*
>
> Luke 10:19

God has given you POWER over the enemy, and by now you know that poverty is clearly one of the tools the enemy uses to keep us weak and ineffective.

But, you have the POWER TO OVERCOME POVERTY. It is part of your prosperity heritage as a son or daughter of the Most High God.

> *Forasmuch then as the children are partakers of flesh and blood, he also himself likewise took part of the same; that through death he might destroy HIM THAT HAD THE POWER of death, ... the devil;*
>
> Hebrew 2:14

Child of God, look at that carefully: The devil HAD the power, but today, HE IS DESTROYED. The devil's power to keep you sick, poor, tired – have all been wiped out. God is calling you now to be a **great giver** in every aspect of the endtime harvest.

And, as strange as it may seem, you are now beginning to see that this wonderful truth about abundance is not just the impossible dream, but it is a real thing that is now happening to you. You are possessing a new prosperity mentality. You are walking out of the door of financial **impossibilities** and into the door of unlimited financial **possibilities** through the power of God!

Lesson 82: Re-claiming your lost treasures

Think of how much more properous you would be right now if you could only reclaim those treasures in life that you've previously lost.

You may have stepped out in faith to be a missionary, only to lose your house and property in the process.

Maybe you have gone through painful divorces, and "lost everything."

Perhaps you have been the victim of alcoholism or drugs, and have been fired from your job, or even lost your home and family.

Maybe you have not been repaid the money you loaned, or the lawyer or accountant you trusted proved to be dishonest.

God, in His Loving concern for you, and as part of the prosperity process, has provided you with a SPIRITUAL WAY to reclaim these lost treasures. God demands double restitution!

> *If a man shall deliver unto his neighbor money or stuff to keep, and it be stolen out of the man's house;* IF THE THIEF BE FOUND, LET HIM PAY DOUBLE.
>
> *Exodus 22: 7*

Now I know some of you are thinking: "Alright, Brother John, that's all well and good, but I have no idea where that crooked attorney is anymore. He's left the state, and no one knows where he's at."

Do not worry. We must focus on the true culprit behind these robberies, no matter what was stolen.

The attorney, the liquor, the drugs are not the thief. Child of God, the engineer of your robbery is Satan himself! He works in the children of disobedience – unsaved men and women.

> *Wherein in time past ye walked according to the course of this world, according to the prince of the power of the air, the spirit **that now worketh in the children of disobedience**.*
>
> *Ephesians 2:2*

The devil is the TRUE THIEF; he is the one who takes what belongs to you, whether it be your health, your wealth, your happiness, your job, or other possessions. But, the Bible says if you FIND THE THIEF, and accuse him, you will receive DOUBLE what you lost!

Child of God, you have found the thief – Satan himself. You are not wrestling with flesh and blood lawyers, bankers, real estate agents, or any other profession, you are wrestling with Satan and

140

his staff of demon forces.

The next move is up to you. God is waiting for His people to take up the TOOLS He has already provided us, the WEAPONS OF OUR SPIRITUAL WARFARE, and take back all that has been taken from us.

The very important principles of reclaiming our ripped off possessions are clearly taught in my book entitled, **Stolen Property Returned.** You can take back what Satan has stolen from you; my book tells you how, step-by-step.

WHO IS BEHIND YOUR POVERTY?

IN SUMMARY

Behind every evil activity on this earth there is a single mastermind: Satan himself. He is behind all the troubles, sicknesses, disappointments, robberies, and poverty that took place in the past, and STILL are happening today!

When you name Satan in your spiritual warfare, and take the true villain – the devil – to God's heavenly court, then you can begin to unlock God's system of retribution and restoration in your life.

Peter knew how to see past the flesh and go right to the source of the problem.

In Acts 5:1-11, we have the example of Ananias and his wife, Sapphira. Together, they secretly plotted to gain prestige among their Christian brothers and sisters. They decided they could have the same prestige as Barnabas received when he gave the total selling price of a piece of land to the work of God. Yet, they thought they could deceive Peter and keep a portion of the money for themselves.

But Peter put the ax to the root of this lying deception by confronting the REAL LIAR:

Why hath Satan filled thine heart to lie.

Acts 5:3a

Peter knew the enemy – Satan – and boldly took him to the heavenly courtroom of God. As a result, both Ananias and Sapphira received immediate judgment for allowing the enemy of God to operate through them.

Remember, the devil is the root of all sin (lies, etc.), but Jesus is the root of righteousness. Your environment is not able to keep you from prospering when you follow God's laws of biblical economics.

141

If your life is in poverty, it is not because of some chance of birth, education, ethnic origin, or whatever you think is holding you back.

Your battle and problems are with the devil, and with yourself. If God gives you the POWER to get wealth, then it logically follows that Satan holds the power to bring poverty.

To begin now to live a prosperous life, start challenging the real source of your problem – the devil, your own inconsistencies, even laziness, and – ACCUSE the devil in God's heavenly court. Demand your goods back, and rebuke him from your thinking patterns; think only on the things God says in His Word concerning you and your prosperity.

Be strong-handed when dealing with the devil, and if you can see any traces of laziness in you, purge them out of your life with the same violence and energy you use on the devil!

Poverty cannot live when you destroy the root causes.

SECTION TWELVE: SEVEN FINAL STEPS TO PROSPERITY!

Lesson 83: Step 1: Give, expecting to receive

No matter how well you understand the Principles of Biblical Economics discussed in this book, understanding alone is not enough to unleash God's prosperity in your life.

Contrary to common belief, the Bible does not say "the truth will set you free,"–period! The Scripture does, however, say that "Ye shall know the truth, and the truth shall make you free," (John 8:32). The word translated "know" goes beyond the most common usage of the word "to know." Here, it means "to go beyond head knowledge," and speaks of a person who actually is walking in the truth, and is being set free by the truth he knows and does.

At this point of our study, you no doubt understand that giving is the first step to God's abundance in your life. You KNOW this is not just done by knowing the words, but through your actual giving. (If you still do not have a strong conviction that these principles work, I suggest you go back about 20 lessons and take another look at each of these biblical principles).

God's greatest act of giving was done with full expectation of receiving something back. Your Creator gave His most precious Son, Jesus Christ, to die because He knew He would receive sons and daughters in return.

> *For God so loved the world, that he gave his only begotten Son, that whosoever believeth in him should not perish, but have everlasting life.*
>
> *John 3:16*

I hope by now, you have already planted a liberal field of money seeds "in the name of Jesus." Now, expect to receive a money harvest back from each and every seed you planted.

Some would say, "But Brother John, that just doesn't sit well with me. When I give to God, I do not expect anything in return."

Child of God, whether you expect it or not, God will not change His Laws to agree with everyone. You give money seeds, and you will reap a money harvest. When you sow deeds of kindness, you will reap deeds of kindness, because the Bible clearly states that you get back what you give:

*Be not deceived: God is not mocked, for whatsoever a
man soweth, that shall he also reap.*

Galatians 6:7

So, if you have believed God's Word and planted money seeds,
keep on believing God's Word that you will receive a money
harvest! God's Word says that we will reap **if** we faint not:

*And let us not be weary in well doing: for in due
season we shall reap, if we faint not.*

Galatians 6:9

Isn't that wonderful? You can give, expecting a harvest! Since
you can expect a harvest, you can be planning the strategic planting of even more money seeds from your coming money harvest.
Think of it! You can have a perpetual harvest if you have faith for
perpetual seeding.

Remember, seed time and harvest are guaranteed in God's
Word.

Lesson 84: Step Two: Bank on God's Promises

Every day you see and hear the various commercial banks
waging economic war with their competitors. They buy advertising
time on radio, television, and in the newspapers, trying to offer just
the right promise to get you to deposit your money in their bank.

Some offer high interest.

Others offer no charge on your checking accounts.

Still others offer toasters, cookbooks, and yes, even Cabbage
Patch Dolls—just to lure you to their institution.

But, without exception, God offers you the best banking program ever heard of. Hear how attractive it sounds from The Living
Bible.

*But remember this—if you give little, you will get
little. A farmer who plants just a few seeds will get
only a small crop, but if he plants much, he will reap
much. Everyone must make up his own mind as to
how much he should give. Don't force anyone to give
more than he really wants to, for cheerful givers are
the ones God prizes. **God is able to make it up to you
by giving you everything you need and more,** so
that there will **not only be enough for your own
needs, but plenty left over to give joyfully to others.** It is as the Scriptures say: . . .*

*For God, who gives seed to the farmer to plant, and later on, good crops to harvest and eat, **will give you more and more seed to plant and will make it grow so that you can give away more and more fruit from your harvest.***

Yes, God will give you much so that you can give away much.

2 Corinthians 9: 6-11a TLB

Now that you are putting your money in God's bank, you can begin to expect to receive God's promises which promise everything you need and more.

You literally cannot give away too much money when you give in the Name of the Lord. Each time you give an offering, it will be returned to you, multiplied. Just as an earthly banker knows the world's secrets of abundance, you, as a spiritual banker, now know God's secrets of abundance, and can literally **bank** on God, and on His promises, and He will see that you have abundant treasures in heaven and on the earth (even more than enough).

Lesson 85: Step Three: Choose faith over fear

The only way the devil can stop you from receiving your God-ordained portion of wealth is by getting you to accept his deceptive, destructive lies about your inability to breakthrough into abundance, and by making you so fearful of failing you stop your new found liberty in giving.

Satan will desperately try and convince you that your giving is a foolish thing to do, and his deception is rooted in fear. The devil will desperately try to put fear-filled lies into your mind, hoping they will grow like weeds and destroy your much-desired harvest.

Do not be confused as to the origin of fear, as it does not come from God.

For God hath not given us the spirit of fear, but of POWER, and of love, and of a sound mind.

2 Timothy 1:7

God does not want you to operate in fear, but in POWER. Remember, God's heritage for you in Deuteronomy 8:18:

But thou shalt remember the Lord thy God: for it is he that giveth the POWER to get wealth.

You see, God not only gives you the POWER over fear, but He also freely gives you the POWER to get wealth! What a loving God we serve!

God's way to conquer Satan's relentless, FEARFUL lies about your finances, is to have you walk in FAITH. Faith and fear cannot operate together. Neither can doubt and faith work together. They work against each other, and bring about instability and failure.

A double-minded man is unstable in all his ways, James 1:8 says. Reject fear. Reject doubt. Take each step of faith as a way of destroying Satan's attempts to bring poverty into your life, instead of your God-given power to get wealth. Faith will always conquer fear when it is operated in the light of Biblical truth.

Remember, as you become faithful in your finances you, are drawing a double reward to yourself:

1. You will be prospering in the financial realm, and
2. You will be positioning yourself to be endowed with the true riches of God (spiritual power and authority).

> *If therefore ye have not been faithful in the unrighteous mammon, who will commit to your trust the true riches?*
>
> Luke 16:11

Surely you can now see that through your FAITH in God's promises, and your faithful stewardship walk, you will become like the workers in the temple that could be trusted with finances:

> *Howbeit there was no reckoning made with them of the money that was delivered into their hand, **because they dealt faithfully**.*
>
> 2 Kings 22:7

Lesson 86: Step Four: Tithe and give offerings

It should now be firmly rooted in your spirit that God expects you to tithe and give offerings, and you are undoubtedly now faithfully performing both spiritual actions in your life. It is important for you to remember at all times that God does not ask you to give your tithes and offerings to make you poor!

You are tithing to open the windows of heaven.

You are giving offerings so that God will pour out a blessing through the open windows – a blessing that is being measured back to you with the same measure that you have measured it out to Him.

Do not let down in either of these dimensions of giving. Both are necessary for you to make the major spiritual breakthrough in your finances that you so desire.

Both of these actions trigger different sets of promises from God, and each of these promises come to you with God's strong desire to see them accomplished:

For all the promises of God in him are yea, and in him Amen, unto the glory of God by us.

2 Corinthians 1:20

Child of God, all the promises of God are **yes**! Everything God has promised for your life, He will deliver to you. If you meet His conditions, these promises, combined with your faithful seed-faith planting, become the basis for your financial prosperity.

Your tithes and offerings are for God, that's true, but they are also the physical actions which release God's abundance into your life from His Heavenly storehouse.

So continue to faithfully give your tithes and offerings to the Lord, and then STAND IN FAITH confidently expecting God's promises to come to pass in your life.

Don't let it make a difference in your giving plan if you do not see a sudden increase in your checkbook balance. Don't let it change your plan, even if your budget remains tight for awhile, or even if your electric bill doubles, or two car tires blow out at the same time.

No matter what the circumstances, the tithing and offering process you are now undertaking will be the tool God uses to unleash His financial abundance in your life. And, in time, there will no longer be a wilderness in your finances, but your desert will bloom like a beautiful garden.

It is not because I say so – it is because the Word of God says so! Remember, God said it! I believe it! That makes it so!

When I do it, my actions make it happen to me!

Lesson 87: Step Five: Plant your seed to glorify God

The Biblical principles of economics are now firmly rooted in your mind and (hopefully) in your actions. The Lord's method of seed planting and sowing shatters much of the world's thinking. The world teaches:

1. Get all you can (get every cent you can).
2. Can all you get (save every penny you get).
3. Sit on the can (never spend any of your savings).

In other words, get all you can and HOLD IT. But God has a different way.

> *There is (he) that scattereth, and yet increaseth; and*
> *there is (he) that withholdeth more than is (fitting),*
> *but it tendeth to poverty. The liberal soul shall be*
> *made fat: and he that watereth shall be watered also*
> *himself.*
>
> *Proverbs 11: 24,25*

You have planted your seeds with a cheerful attitude and a good heart to glorify God. **Now** you can expect an abundant harvest. Because you have been generous in your seed planting, God guarantees that you will be prospered, made fat (with goods), watered, and blessed.

That's His promise to you.

When the devil starts to feed you his lies of fear and pending shortage, remember to "cast down these evil imaginations," and once again stand on the promises of God. You have seen them repeated again and again on the pages of this book, because God says repetition is good for us and He has created our minds to learn things line upon line and precept upon precept.

Remember, you live in a constant barrage of the devil's lying precepts every day of your life: while you might not clearly see them as lies – their total overall effect is strong, and they make a strong impression on your subconscious mind, so in this book I have tried to give equal time to God's Truths.

> *Be not deceived; God is not mocked: for whatsoever a*
> *man soweth, that shall he also reap.*
>
> *Galatians 6:7*

I have sown Biblical seeds of prosperity into your mind, and now that you are planting your financial crop, you will, upon the authority of God's word soon be reaping an ever-increasing harvest so you can have everything you need and plenty left over to effectively finance His endtime harvest.

> *God is able to make it up to you by giving you every-*
> *thing you need and more, so that there will not only*
> *be enough for your own needs, but plenty left over to*
> *give joyfully to others.*
>
> *2 Corinthians 9: 8 TLB*

Lesson 88: Step Six: Reap your harvest

The circumstances in your life may not show any sudden changes. Your finances may still be tight. The bills may still be difficult to pay. You probably do not yet fully see God's blessings in such great abundance in your life that your every need and want are met.

But, child of God, stand on His promises. You are tithing to keep the windows of heaven open, and you are giving offerings to establish a healthy, abundant flow through the windows of heaven.

How many Christians have you heard to say, "Can you help me. I don't **FEEL** saved."

They have believed the words of salvation, they accepted Jesus, but somewhere in their walk they let Satan's lies temporarily cause them to doubt and now they are seeking for assurance from others that they are saved.

"Well," they say, "maybe I should repeat John 3:16 and the sinner's prayer again, just to be sure."

Child of God, have you ever heard that? Have you ever had someone say that to you?

Well, child of God, get ready. Satan will probably throw some stupid lies at you concerning your soon-coming harvest. He will lie and say something like this: "You gave that big offering last week, and what did it get you? You still don't have anything. This is all just a great big mistake."

Stop thinking that before you end up in the poorhouse.

Learn to recognize these lies, and cast them out. Do not give attention to anything that exalts itself against the knowledge of God. These fear tactics are the only means the devil has to try and stop your pending financial harvest.

You gave, according to God's word, and you **will reap** a harvest according to God's word. As sure as God's word is true, and we know it is, your harvest is even now beginning to manifest itself.

Remember, God's word guarantees your harvest. Think about it. When the United States government guarantees the price of a crop, the farmers plant all their fields with that crop, faithfully trusting the government to keep its promise.

How much more can the sons and daughters of God trust Him and plant with confidence, knowing that He will give us the harvest He promises.

Sow your seeds in faith and believe the God of Faith to deliver the promised harvest.

Lesson 89: Step Seven: Always replant a portion of every harvest you reap!

As your financial harvest starts manifesting itself in your life, it isn't always immediately identifiable. Remember that years of traditional thinking have made it easy for you to mistakingly think of the bank or maybe your job as being your source.

Keep your eyes open. Watch for God's blessings, since they may come without clearly being recognized as your much-awaited harvest from God for seeds you planted months ago!

You might catch yourself saying: "Boy, my business is going great lately," or "Hey, my boss just gave me an unexpected raise," or "Man, that new bank did some marvelous things with my investments."

Part of your continuing success process in effectively applying God's Laws of Biblical economics is dependent upon your recognition of the fact that God is your source. It is God that supplies all the needs of His children.

With every upward motion in your finances, learn to say: "Thank you Lord. I recognize this as part of your blessing process that my scriptural giving has released in my life, and I give you the honor and the glory for the harvest you are now manifesting in my financial matters."

When you recognize the Source of your every blessing, then you will recognize your need to continue with the next step – the replanting of some of every increase into the fields of God for the NEXT HARVEST.

If the devil first fails in his attempts to stop you from giving by putting strong doubts about God's promises in your mind, his second deception is even more subtle: he simply tries to cloud the source of increases in your funds, so you will forget to plant new seeds from your abundance. He knows you will plant if you remember God is the source, so he attempts to distract you with garbage about your boss or your bank or even your own business ability really being your source.

Child of God, simply tithe **and** give generous offerings on all income you receive: Your income tax refunds, extra income, virtually any money you receive. Don't allow any room for discretion or doubt.

If a stranger comes up and hands you $10, thank the Lord, tithe a dollar, and give a portion away in an offering to God.

150

Cast down evil imaginations that creep in and push the Spirit of God aside. Keep a healthy planting of seed from your new harvests.

Remember, the paramount truth is that you must plant with regularity if you wish to reap with regularity.

Lesson 90: Let me hear from you!

Child of God, I am excited for you, and for the Kingdom of God.

I know this book has touched your life, or you would not be reading this final page. You have dared to believe God's Word enough to read this far, and I am sure you have already put these Principles of Biblical Economics to work in your life.

So I'm excited. God's excited. And I'm sure you're excited.

When God does pour out blessings on your life – and He will – please write to me and share the good news, the victory reports. I want to hear about the marvelous blessings God is giving in your life. Send me pictures of your new car . . . let me see your new home, tell me about the college to which you are now able to send your son or daughter. Most importantly, **share with me the various ministry outreaches, and the mighty spiritual projects you have been able to help – with your new financial harvest**.

Child of God, God cares about you, and so do I. You see, I didn't write this book for my benefit; I wrote it for yours. So now, take a few moments and write back to me and share what God is doing in your life.

If you want to continue to grow into even deeper understandings of Biblical Principles of Economics, I've included in the last few pages of this book some of the most powerful tapes and books you will find anywhere. God has put an anointing on my life to teach these and other Biblical principles, and I believe you will find information in these books and tapes that are unique Biblical truths.

God bless you abundantly as you continue to develop these powerful truths that will enable you to be an effective part in financing the endtime harvest – God's Way!

Order These Vital Books
By
Dr. Avanzini
Today

Over 500,000 copies are already sold!

Always Abounding   **$5.00 U.S.A.**
This anointed book brings you into the daily, practical areas of giving and receiving, sowing and reaping — in a way that will seem like a whole new theology to many. But, every concept is founded on the Word. You must have this book!

Stolen Property Returned!   **$6.00 U.S.A.**
This book has already changed thousands of lives! You have been ripped off by the most successful thief in the history of the universe — Satan. In this book, you will learn how to TAKE BACK WHAT SATAN HAS STOLEN. Learn how to regain your lost possessions, lost loved ones, lost reputation . . . literally anything that has been snatched from you by the devil. If you have ever lost anything to Satan, this book is a must for you.

Financing the Endtime Harvest — God's Way
"Ninety Lessons and Twelve Summaries in the Principles of Biblical Economics"   **$7.00 U.S.A.**
God intends for His people to have "more than enough." To reap the final endtime harvest of souls, there must be major financial breakthroughs in the body of Christ.

Learn how you can BE A BLESSING TO others through these 90 powerful lessons on the Biblical Principles of Economics.

The Wealth of the Wicked "Is Laid Up for the Just"
                                        $7.00 U.S.A.
This total Biblical revelation of the great endtime transfer of the wealth of the wicked rich into the hands of God's children is without a doubt the greatest revelation pertaining to finances in the church today. This book is a non-speculative Biblical documentary of the little known Bible teaching pertaining to the vast stockpile of wealth that the wicked systematically hoard, that God regularly takes from them and redistributes to His informed children. The book also proves from scripture that the time of the final and greatest transfer of this wealth has already started.

NOTES

NOTES

NOTES